Making Your Mark

Mark Mills

MAKING YOUR MARK

How I built a fortune from £1.50 – and you can too

Harriman House

HARRIMAN HOUSE LTD
18 College Street
Petersfield
Hampshire
GU31 4AD
GREAT BRITAIN
Tel: +44 (0)1730 233870

Email: enquiries@harriman-house.com
Website: www.harriman-house.com
First published in Great Britain in 2019
Copyright © Mark Mills

Hardback ISBN: 978-0-85719-778-8
eBook ISBN: 978-0-85719-779-5

British Library Cataloguing in Publication Data
A CIP catalogue record for this book can be obtained from the British Library.

With thanks to my parents, John and Leoni,
my brothers, Andrew and Nigel,
especially my children, Oliver, Christian and Isabella,
but most of all, my wife Angela.

Contents

About Mark Mills

Mark Mills has built and sold numerous businesses for himself and with other people.

He built Europe's largest independent cash machine company, Cardpoint plc., which at its peak was dispensing more than £500m each month. Prior to Cardpoint, Mark was an early disruptor in the postal industry, developing an advertising-fronted postbox and installing 1,200 at petrol stations throughout the UK, making it the only other postbox network to rival the Royal Mail.

Mark is a committed family man and is married to his patient, understanding wife, Angela, and has three grown-up children, Oliver, and twins Christian and Isabella. They have all supported Mark in his efforts, whether successful or otherwise. Mark still lives where he was born on the outskirts of Blackpool and believes you should never forget where you came from.

Introduction

There's a well-known phrase that I use all the time, adding my own twist at the end – *been there, done that, got the T-shirt and the scars underneath*. I think it perfectly sums up the experience of creating a successful business. It may seem easy from the outside, but if you look beneath the surface, achieving success usually turns out to have involved an enormous amount of effort – much of it painful.

There's little better in life than making your mark. But it also leaves a mark on you.

While starting and growing a business from scratch can be extremely rewarding, it can also be a lonely struggle. A lot of the time you are on your own trying to figure out what to do and how to do it. Every day you have to make big decisions simply to keep the business moving forward, some of which will turn out to be right, others of which will turn out to be wrong. You can ask advice from as many people as you want. But at the end of the day, your business matters most to one person: you. Other people simply can't care about it as much.

It is down to you, and you alone, to make it work.

I've been on that journey. I started out with nothing but eventually achieved fantastic success with my cash machine business, Cardpoint. At its peak it had 6,500 cash machines and 300 employees and was worth £170m. But my success didn't happen overnight. It wasn't easy. It took me many years of hard work and persistence before I made it. And there were plenty of setbacks and challenges to overcome.

I decided to write this book because I wanted to tell the real inside story of my success – not just the glittering rewards and accolades at the end, but the hard graft along the way. I wanted to explain how I got from there to here, scars and all, in the hope that it might help and inspire other people to do the same.

The truth is that setting up and growing a business does not always go according to plan. In fact, it rarely does. There is no guarantee that it's all going to work out well the first time, or even the second or third. Things are inevitably going to go wrong. But here's the thing – that's fine. It's natural and to be expected, and it's all part of the adventure. You just have to accept that – even embrace it – because it's during the tough times that you learn the most important lessons and ultimately find out what you are really made of.

No matter what stage you are at in life or business, I hope that my story will help you understand that you are not alone, and that it is OK to take the long way round to success. You don't have to get it right the first time. You just have to keep on doing the right thing until it produces great results. Success comes from persistence – and it's worth persisting because success takes you to places you could never imagine.

For me, that has included a garden party at Buckingham Palace, meetings at the heart of government, a visit inside a top-secret nuclear submarine and trips all around the world, including to China, Thailand, India and South Africa. It has also provided me with many unusual experiences, including being on *News at Ten*, a hot air balloon landing in my garden, a court case in the High Court in London and trips on many private jets, to name but a few. Oh, and there was almost a near-death experience…

There is one more reason for writing this book. I have a letter on the wall of my office from Bill Clinton. I wrote to him to tell him how much I enjoyed reading his autobiography, *My Life*, and a few weeks later he wrote back, thanking me for my interest in his work and expressing his best wishes for finishing my own book.

There was no way I was going to let the former president of the United States down, so here it is.

I hope you enjoy it and find it useful.

How it all Started

I discovered the thrill of being an entrepreneur at the age of eight. My aunt worked in the Burton's biscuit factory near where we lived and every Thursday she would bring round a large bag of broken biscuits to our house. I quickly realised that this could be an opportunity to make some money: I divided the biscuits into small bags and took them into school the next day to sell at break time for 10p a bag. My friends would wait anxiously all week to spend their pocket money on these biscuits – I would usually sell out by the end of first break on Friday.

I suppose I could have simply given the biscuits away, but to me it was much more exciting to try and make some money. I still remember the buzz. I made around £3 a week in sales, pure profit – and a fortune for an eight-year-old back then. My love affair with business had begun.

I grew up in Lytham St Annes, a seaside town in Lancashire, where I lived in a semi-detached house with my parents, my twin brother Andy and my older brother Nigel.

My dad ran a glazing business and would come home for lunch every day. He was quite content to keep his business small and local, and we would joke that whenever he left Lytham St Annes to go to Kirkham (the next town, five miles away) he would need to take his map, flask and sandwich box with him. Mum was a secretary and to our huge embarrassment worked at our primary school for a while. Fortunately for us kids, she moved on to another job quite quickly.

After the success of selling the broken biscuits, I was keen to try and make money by selling something else. I began to make bags of popcorn. I would give my mother the money I had made from the biscuits to buy the kernels and then I would ruin many pans perfecting my corn-popping technique at home, before sprinkling the finished product with sugar and putting it in small plastic bags. I also sold bags of broken rock after discovering a local rock factory based in an old St John's Ambulance station nearby. None of my friends knew that the factory was there, so they also didn't know that I bought the bags for just 15p each and then sold them for £1.

I was amazed at how much profit I was able to make on each bag, and kept on selling the rock all the way through junior school. The only downside was I ate so much rock myself that I ended up needing quite a number of dental fillings when I was older.

By the time I started senior school – a private school called King Edward VII's in Lytham St Annes – I was constantly on the lookout for new ways to make money. It was not long before I came up with a really lucrative idea. At the time, my friend and I loved eating a snack called Wheat Crunchies, but the school tuck shop didn't sell them because they weren't stocked by their regular supplier. However, my father had joined the local cash-and-carry supermarket in order to buy cheap groceries for the family, so I managed to persuade him to buy boxes of Wheat Crunchies for me at the same time. I started supplying them to the school tuck shop for a healthy profit. There was an additional benefit to this arrangement– I became friendly with the caretaker who ran the tuck shop and he would give me a discount on anything I bought from him.

Additionally, I was tall for my age and looked older than I was, so I was able to buy magazines of *special interest*, such as *Playboy* and *Penthouse*. I would then sell them on to my friends who hadn't been able to buy the magazines themselves – for twice the price.

Every month I would buy them in bulk from a newsagent about a mile away from home, to ensure that I wouldn't bump into anyone I knew. I would then hide the magazines at home until I was able to pass them on to my friends. One day I bought the whole top shelf. As I put them on the counter the shopkeeper smiled and said, "You are in for a good night!" I certainly was, but perhaps not in the way he imagined. I was thinking of the profit.

By far my most successful business venture while at school, though, was organising parties for sixth formers. When kids turned 14, some parents would let them hold parties at home, but by the time they turned 15 or 16, most of these parents were fed up of having their houses trashed and so refused to allow them to hold them at home anymore. But my friends and I still wanted to have fun, so there was a real demand for some way to hold a private party.

I quickly realised that this could be an opportunity to make money. I went along to a local night club called The Attic at Blackpool Pleasure Beach with my best friend Jeremy and met the manager, Stuart. The Attic was not a high-class venue – it was mostly frequented by holiday makers and people who couldn't get in anywhere else. I told the manager that I wanted to organise a party for my friends. A bunch of sixth formers aged 16 and 17 were clearly not going to meet the nightclub's over-18 age requirement, but we didn't dwell on this. After some negotiation he agreed to sell me a book of 300 entrance tickets. He stamped them all with a date in July and charged me a total of £5 for the lot.

I then sold the tickets for 50p each to sixth formers at my all-boys school and at the girls' school next door. It took some guts to walk round to the girls' school and ask the head girl if she would like to be my ticket agent, but it certainly made me popular.

I turned up at the nightclub early on the night of the party and reminded Stuart the manager of our arrangement. He did not remember me. I decided not to panic and spent the next ten minutes trying to convince him that a couple of hundred sixth formers were about to show up, ready to party and with money to spend. The nightclub was completely empty apart from the two of us. He clearly didn't believe me.

Thirty minutes later, he did. At 9pm on the dot people arrived in large groups and the bar was soon so busy with drinks orders that I was drafted in to pull pints. Meanwhile, Stuart was on the phone trying to persuade more staff to come in as quickly as possible to help out. He looked very stressed.

By the end of the evening, I was Stuart's new best friend because his sales figures had just leapt through the roof. The party had been a roaring success and he enthusiastically encouraged me to organise more.

My school friends thought it was a success, too, and badgered me to organise more. They had no idea that I was making a profit from them – they thought that I was paying the club owner to let me host the parties. I didn't tell them otherwise.

I started organising monthly parties at The Attic, increasing the price to £3 a ticket. Even at this price the tickets sold straightaway, and the parties were so popular that other local schools began to copy us and hold their own parties there. Parents were actually happy; their homes were not getting trashed.

The venture wasn't without its hiccups. One evening I was called into Stuart's office to find the local chief constable there with two of his police officers, berating Stuart for allowing under-age drinking in his nightclub.

I spoke to the police to try to defuse the situation and then went back into the club and told everyone that the police were here to arrest any underage drinkers. But nobody believed me. They thought it was a wind-up. (It didn't help that I had pulled such a practical joke before, only letting everyone in on the joke once they had fled outside into the cold.) This time it was for real. I found my twin brother – sandwiched between two girls – and we left immediately.

Fortunately, nobody got into any trouble. As soon as the first policeman appeared, everyone disappeared. The occasion went down in history as everyone's first brush with the law – and a lucky escape.

The pinnacle of the Attic Parties, as they were known, was the New Year's Eve party of 1987. This time, as tickets were in great demand, I increased the price to £5 and managed to get about 400 people in, 200 of whom were from the girls' school.

They had all bought their tickets from the girl I'd recruited to help me. When she arrived she handed me a carrier bag containing £1,000 in notes and coins. I spent the evening with the money weighing down my pockets because I had nowhere else to put it. At one point, whilst dancing enthusiastically in a drunken haze, about £20 in pound coins fell out of my pockets all over the dance floor, never to be seen again. That soon sobered me up. The girl who acted as my ticket agent, incidentally, has since gone on to become a successful police officer.

Stuart, the manager, also held a raffle and I won a meal for me and my then girlfriend for Valentine's night at the very salubrious White Tower Restaurant at the Pleasure Beach.

When I left school, I handed over the organisation of the Attic Parties to a friend in the year below, who continued to hold them for several years afterwards.

All in all, a great business.

Leaving school was less successful. On our last day of school, I realised that we had done nothing to mark the occasion, so I stood on the pool table in the common room and suggested that we throw a teacher into the nearby lake.

My brother fetched our mother's car – a Morris Ital in beige and hardly a sex machine, but we appreciated the use of it – and we kidnapped the youngest teacher, Mr Fuller. Then we drove down to the lakeside and, after taking him by a leg and an arm, threw him into the lake, with everyone taking photos, cheering and laughing. He took it very well, but as my brother and I were the ringleaders, the headmaster wrote to my parents and warned them that if there were any further incidents of this kind, he would be obliged to either take the matter to court, or exclude us from taking our exams at the school.

Our parents were so cross that they told us we had been expelled. I only found out the truth 30 years later when I discovered the letter the headmaster had sent to them. I didn't know either that when the teacher landed in the lake, he hurt his back.

Sorry Mr Fuller!

Perhaps because of all the other things I was doing, I didn't do very well in my A Levels, only passing two of them, French and Economics. I completely failed German. I did receive an offer from Stirling University to do a degree in Business Law but, after giving it some thought, I decided not to go and instead start trying to earn a living in business. My parents were not that pleased about my decision, but they could see that it was something I really wanted to do, so they didn't stand in my way.

My Grandpa Ron was only too happy to help me get started. He and my Grandma Anne were forever trying to make money from various business ventures. While I was growing up, they would sign up for every home-selling scheme going, from Tupperware to oil paintings and voucher schemes. They were quite convinced that every one of these schemes was going to make them better off. Often when I went round to their house, I would find their small cul-de-sac full of cars. Inside there would be 20 to 30 people packed into their lounge, drinking tea and eating biscuits while my grandparents demonstrated the latest vegetable chopper and outlined the health benefits they had enjoyed from it, or showed off water filters designed to make you live longer, or oil paintings to adorn your home.

Sadly, most of their schemes didn't work, but it never dimmed their enthusiasm. When things didn't work out and they were left with stock, they either used it or gave it away, simply moving on to the next big idea that always seemed just around the corner.

When I announced that I was going into business rather than going to university, Grandpa Ron offered to go into business with me. He told me that he had seen some cleaning cloths called Miracle Cloths in *Exchange and Mart* magazine that he thought could make us some money. The cloths promised to clean almost anything, and so Grandpa provided £300 for us to buy thousands of them. Every morning I would pick a town at random and drive there in my mum's car, then I would walk the streets asking retailers if they would like to buy some Miracle Cloths to sell in their shop. To help convince them, I would do a demonstration of the cloth's ability to take stains off anything from bikes to jewellery. There was the occasional mishap, however – I once demonstrated the cloth on a white PVC window that my dad was installing and it stained the frame yellow, which he wasn't over the moon about.

I managed to sell around two dozen cloths a day, but it was hard work and my heart wasn't really in it, so in the end we sold them all to one big retailer. However, it did make me realise that if you walk round long enough and talk to enough people, somebody will eventually buy something from you.

My grandpa and I then decided to try and sell water filters, but that didn't go too well either. We also tried setting up a voucher scheme for hairdressers, but it soon became clear that that wasn't going to make our fortune.

For my next venture I decided to go it alone. I grandly announced to my bemused parents that I was going into business on my own and had bought a newly formed and ready-to-trade company called Prestige Communication Corporation Limited for £85.

Through someone I met while selling water filters, I had discovered that the market for payphones was opening up, as a result of the liberalisation of British Telecom, which meant that anyone could supply payphones, not just BT. I realised that this could be the business opportunity I had been waiting for.

My GOLDEN RULES for thinking like an entrepreneur

Aim to take away the hassle

My wife once asked me: *how do you make money? You haven't got a degree, you have taught yourself about business and yet we live in a massive house with nice cars. How is that?* I told her that I had distilled it down to one word: hassle. If you want to build a house, you could build it yourself: go on a course to learn bricklaying and plumbing and buy a machine to cut wood and make windows. Alternatively, you could pay a builder, who will take all that hassle away from you and build the house. In the same way, you could make your own sandwich every morning, or you could just nip to the sandwich shop and pay someone else £3 to take on the hassle of buying the bread and ham and butter and make a sandwich for you. You could iron your own shirts, or you could pay someone £1.50 a shirt to iron them for you and take away the hassle. They make a living, and you are free to spend your evenings watching TV with your family, rather than doing things others are happy to do for you. At its core, all business models are based on the idea of taking hassle away from someone. To find a good idea for a business, you just need to think about where people are feeling hassled in their lives, and how you might be able to take that hassle away from them by doing the work yourself.

Make your business a priority

When I was 20, I was so obsessed with the idea of creating a successful business that after lunch on Christmas Day I ducked out of watching the Queen's Speech and *Only Fools and Horses* and went to my office instead. I had loads of stuff to do and it felt like an ideal moment to do it. I spent a happy few hours on my own there creating a mailshot until the office phone rang. It was my mother calling in a panic because no one knew where I had gone. She had called my flat and rung all my friends and even sent someone out to look for me. She just couldn't understand why on earth I would choose to work on Christmas Day. But to me it made perfect sense.

Never give in

However many calls you have to make, customers you have to see, ideas you have to try, keep going. It will work in the end.

The Prestige Years

My business idea was to provide payphones to retailers for less money than it would cost them to buy a BT payphone. I found a supplier of non-BT payphones which I thought could work well. Firstly, because they only needed an ordinary phone line, unlike BT payphones, which would save retailers the cost of installing a special 'payphone' line. Secondly, because these payphones, again, unlike BT Payphones, took a range of coins and didn't give change. This meant that if customers didn't have the right coins, they might have to use a 50p coin for a 10p call, thereby increasing the profit for the retailer.

Next, I found a shop to rent for £50 a week advertised in the local paper. When I went to view it, it still displayed the sign put up by the previous occupant, which said 'Fresh and Fruity', so the business was known as this until I could afford to replace the sign.

To my parents' horror, I also persuaded my eldest brother Nigel to leave his secure and hard-won job at British Aerospace to join me in business. Andy, my twin, joined later to look after the accounts side of the business – so we had sales, installations and accounts covered.

I knew the only way to find potential customers was to cold-call them, so I phoned pubs, restaurants, cafés and petrol stations – anywhere that was run by an owner-manager who could make an instant decision. If they sounded interested, I would arrange to visit them.

I found a lucrative market in social clubs, many of whom liked the idea of saving money on their payphone. Instead of selling our payphones outright, we sold them on seven-year leases through a leasing company, which gave us up to £1,000 upfront for every lease signed. We were responsible for the maintenance of the phones too, but there were few moving parts so there wasn't much that could go wrong.

I quickly discovered that I needed to make 100 cold-calls to retailers in order to achieve a single sale. There were no shortcuts to success. Making the calls never got easier, but it did work. I knew that if I did my 500 calls each week, I would sell five phones.

I quickly learned to understand, embrace even, the rejection involved in selling this way; in my mind, I framed each 'no' as being one person closer to a 'yes'. I knew I needed 99 people to say 'no' before I made a payphone sale, so I would zip through my 100 calls each day, almost hoping for a 'no', so that the 'yes' would come around quicker. I realised that having a thick skin in business was more than helpful, it was essential. These days, I describe myself as bulletproof.

Constant cold-calling did have one side benefit though. Being told 'no' 495 times a week made asking girls out on dates a lot easier, as the prospect of rejection no longer bothered me. I realised that even if nine out of ten girls said 'no', there was likely to be one who said 'yes'. As a result, I had a lot more fun than my bashful friends did.

I gradually developed a convincing way to sell the payphones. I wrote a cost comparison sheet, which I'd now call a profit comparison sheet, to show each retailer how much their BT payphone was costing them compared to how much our payphones would earn them.

Our unique selling point was that BT was charging the retailer the equivalent of 7.39p per 10p call, rather than the 4.4p our phones charged, giving them a measly 26.1% profit margin compared to our 56%. Each time I managed to show the retailer my cost comparison sheet, I almost always sold them a payphone.

Years later, a salesman came to work for us from a competitor and, in his sales presentation, he actually had a cost comparison sheet from a retailer that I'd filled out. I took that as a compliment.

As the business grew, we constantly tried to recruit employees. This didn't always work out. Once, I had arranged to interview a potential employee at a motorway service station near Bristol and, as I walked up the steps to meet him, the heel of my shoe fell off. I tried to pretend that I had a limp, but it wasn't the best way to convince someone that they would be earning £1,000 a week working for us. He didn't take the job.

Prestige taught me the most valuable non-financial lesson I've ever learned: that patience and persistence are rewarded. *Never give in –* instead of admitting defeat, simply redirect your efforts.

In 1990, we made our first acquisition. A former colleague of my brother's, from his British Aerospace days, Alastair Richardson, had gone to work for a company called Telecom UK, which wanted to dispose of its UK business (based in Preston). We were undoubtedly the best candidates to buy.

We didn't pay much for the business, instead taking over several liabilities. In particular, the staff. Unfortunately, many lacked the drive to become a part of our business and were let go. One exception to this was Alastair Richardson, who helped move the company to Blackpool. This involved us borrowing my father's Luton Bedford van and driving to and from Preston all night, loading and unloading chairs, desks, computers and equipment. We must have driven between the two business parks 15 times that night – and they were 25 miles apart. It didn't give me much faith in the local police force, as they never noticed what could have been highly suspicious movements of a van with the words 'St Annes Glass' on the side.

We also briefly became the owner of a false ceiling. The leased building that Telecom UK occupied made no mention of a false ceiling, which had been put in after they moved in, but we decided that it now belonged to us. Then, one of our customers happened to mention that he needed a ceiling for the restaurant in the hotel he owned, and so a week or two later we delivered the false ceiling, tiles and dividers to him in return for £500.

After getting rid of the staff the acquisition really paid off, as it meant we picked up some customers, did more business, attracted publicity and learned a lot – all for free.

Our next acquisition was AES Telecom, trading as 'The Phone Box', a husband-and-wife business operating in central Blackpool to sell payphones and telephone systems. The business cost us £3,000 and taught me a valuable lesson. On the day we were to collect their equipment and van, Alastair and I discussed whether we needed additional insurance on the van, or whether we'd be covered third party under our existing insurance. As he left our office Alastair said: "I wouldn't bother with the extra insurance, Mark, I'm hardly likely to crash between there and here."

But a little voice inside me kept saying, "Insure the van! Insure the van!" To me, there didn't seem to be any advantage in relying upon third party cover when I could easily arrange for full coverage before Alastair even arrived to collect the van. So I rang an insurance broker to organise the cover.

Thirty minutes later, Alastair arrived back at the office looking rather sheepish; on his way back to our office with the van he had crashed into another car at a petrol station.

After ten minutes of making Alastair squirm, warning him about jail sentences for uninsured driving and having to re-mortgage his house to pay for the damage to the vehicles, I eventually told him that

I had insured the van. The look of relief on his face was enormous. It taught us both a useful lesson about only taking calculated risks.

By now, we were employing 12 people, as the business had diversified into providing telephone systems.

On one occasion, Nigel and I installed a phone system at a radio station in Blackpool. We did the work overnight because they had a telesales department operating during the day. Arriving at 9pm, we promptly unplugged the phones before starting to wire up the new system. As we worked, we listened to the live show of a DJ produced in the studio next to us, who we noticed was giving out dedications before each song was played. Things like Rebecca saying, "Tony, I love you", or that Dave's parents had called to wish him a happy birthday. When the DJ eventually emerged from his studio at the end of his show, we looked at him in bafflement as the unplugged phones lay at our feet and asked how he managed to get dedications without a working phone line. He just laughed and said he had made it all up.

As the business grew, we started selling mobile phones and were able to move out of our humble rented offices into grander ones. Our good fortune didn't last long, though, as the cash always seemed to be going out of the door before any came in.

A contributing factor was that more competitors came into the market just as the economic climate worsened. Under these conditions, we began to find it harder to bring in new sales. In fact, I would often ring our office number to check that the line was still working. We were still trading profitably, as I only allowed deals to be struck at good margins, but we were soon heading downhill.

We did make a few bad decisions too, none more so than when a man came to buy a mobile phone for his wife to use in the car. At the time, the only people who bought mobile phones were business people, so we genuinely thought the man was mad. We simply couldn't imagine why anyone would want to buy a mobile phone if they weren't using it for business. And as it was clear we were never going to generate enough sales purely by selling to business people, we soon decided to stop selling mobile phones altogether. It was a spectacularly, badly timed decision.

It was also hard to ensure that we were paid. One time, we supplied a hotel refurbishment company with about £7,000 worth of phones, but they would not send payment. I went to their offices and told the receptionist that I'd like to see the finance director, but he sent a message fobbing me off. I was determined not to leave without my money, though, so I told the receptionist that I would wait in their reception area until I was brought my payment.

I waited and waited until, after a few hours, the finance director finally came out of his office. He agreed that payment was overdue and gave me his word that he would post the cheque the following day. It arrived two days later. One week after that, I received a letter saying that his business had gone into liquidation. Our cheque had just cleared in time. That's why you should always listen to your instinct, whatever your advisors, colleagues, customers or staff tell you.

Despite the payment, it was not enough to save Prestige and, in 1991, we had to put the business into administration.

We naively thought that as the money we were owed equalled the money we owed others, that we could simply wrap it up and walk away. However, that was before we had taken into account the advisors' fees, which we were shocked to discover amounted to £20,000. This made the sums look very different.

I'm proud to say that I eventually paid everybody off in full, including the bank, even though it did mean having to live frugally for a few years. During the first years of marriage to Angela (who is still my wife), we couldn't afford to go on holiday or even go out for a meal because every penny I earned went towards paying off the debt. One advantage of that, though, has been that I never doubt Angela's love for me, as she loved me when I was completely broke. When I first took her out I had to borrow a friend's car: I have tried to make up for it ever since.

My GOLDEN RULES for creating a successful business model

Look for recurring revenue

In most businesses there is a version of recurring revenue that will bring you income even when you are not selling, making you resistant to downturns.

Protect the downside

If you have to pay for insurance, pay for it sooner rather than later. If your home or premises aren't alarmed, why wait until you are burgled to spend the money. Get ahead of the game and minimise risk.

Stand in your customers' shoes

When selling goods and services, think hard about what the customer wants to see, hear and feel. It's not about how good you are as a seller, but whether your customer is excited to work with you and whether they think your involvement will make their own business more profitable and fun.

Adventure in Advertising

With no sign of the market improving, it was time to embark on a new business venture.

My twin brother, Andy, had decided to go into business on his own to have his own adventures, leaving our eldest brother, Nigel, and me to the next business. I am glad to say Andy has been successful, a fact that makes me very proud of him.

Over a drink, our printer, Andy Campbell, Nigel and I came up with the idea of publishing a directory of dialling codes. Telephone codes were being altered by the addition of an extra 1 – from 061, 071 to 0161, 0171 – and while BT used to publish a directory, they hadn't done so for many years. We decided to collate the information from various lists of local dialling codes and our own knowledge. We then filled in the blanks from the *Yellow Pages*, as we already owned a directory for every area in the country (buying them from BT for £5 each) due to our payphone business.

We decided to sell adverts on the cover and then provide the directories to households for free. We would create different directories for each area, all with the same dialling code content but with local advertising on the cover.

Our new business, Telecom Publications Limited, or TPL for short, was born. We rented a small office above a shop in Blackpool and appointed Nigel the managing director. While Andy did all the printing, Nigel and I dealt with sales and distribution. More significantly, we secured the telephone number 345678, which was ideal for a business related to telephones and started my passion for branding through numbers. I owned 34% of the business, while Nigel and Andy Campbell had 33% each.

We created a prototype of the directory with made-up adverts and, after choosing Stoke-on-Trent as a starting point, cold-called local businesses there to see if they wanted to advertise in our directory. I sold the first advert to a builders' merchant, who paid £800 to advertise on the back cover for two years.

It was definitely a eureka moment.

We quickly hit a stumbling block, however. When we distributed our dialling code directories, BT saw one of them and thought we had copied the information from their old directory. They decided that they owned the copyright for the list of UK dialling codes and that we couldn't publish it. Their 'cease and desist' notice came by fax and landed on my desk one Friday afternoon, which wasn't a great experience.

We weren't convinced that we couldn't publish, so we employed a solicitor who was a friend-of-a-friend and relatively cheap. This proved to be a mistake. It soon became clear that this solicitor wanted to make his name by taking the case and running with it, proving to BT that he had a fine legal brain and no doubt bankrupting us in the meantime. Fortunately, we quickly realised that this was his plan and so were able to rein him in. To be fair, he actually was a fine legal brain, but I didn't fancy paying for him to prove it.

We eventually settled with BT by both sides agreeing to differ as to whether copyright can subsist in a list and us paying them a nominal sum for a licence to use their list. What BT had failed to realise was that this worked fantastically in our favour, as we could now say to potential clients: "I'm calling from Telecom Publications Limited and we have a licence from BT. We publish the National Dialling Codes Directory…"

We published hundreds of thousands of directories, all the same content inside, just with different, local adverts on the cover.

Whenever I met with potential clients, I would hand over a business card without a job title on it. This was something I had learnt while working at Prestige, as I could be more effective in negotiations if people didn't know that I was the boss. Instead, I found it useful to be able to tell the other side that I had to consult with someone else before agreeing to a deal. It would often buy me extra time or enable me to do a better deal. Or I'd tell customers that I couldn't negotiate a lower price as that was the boss's golden rule – I wasn't lying, and it worked really well.

TPL also showed me the importance of recurring income, the benefits of which we discovered due to a misprint. Advertisers were given the opportunity to pay for their advert in four quarterly instalments yet, in some instances, this was written in the contract simply as quarterly instalments. This meant that some advertisers kept on paying us after they should have stopped.

We repaid the money advertisers had overpaid, but realised that we could amend new contracts to say, in legal terms, that overpayments were deemed to be pre-payments for the future, meaning that we didn't need to repay any money received in this way.

This was a great advantage, as we had effectively 'pre-sold' advertising space ahead of canvassing new advertisers, thus improving our cash flow. We also didn't have to pay tax on the income in the year it came in because it was classed as deferred income.

At its peak, Nigel and I were making about £20,000 each a year from the business. However, the recession in the early 1990s meant many businesses tightened their belts, squeezing our advertising revenue. Eventually we sold the business to Andy for a token £1.

Nigel was given the unenviable job of making everybody redundant. One morning, as each member of staff came into work, Andy would take a person aside and deliver the bad news. But when people started arriving in greater numbers, Nigel couldn't do this fast enough and was forced to shout, "Don't take your coats off!"

By this point, you might think I would start to doubt my ability to run a business. But the experience of creating and running Prestige and TPL had actually encouraged me. When you've dealt with thousands of people, been a managing director and made a few quid, it's completely addictive. You crave achievement and recognition and want to do it all again.

Fortunately, we had already come up with a new business venture, BusinessBoard, based on the principle of getting recurring income from advertising. With the launch of Direct Line insurance, which enabled customers to consult an insurance firm without an intermediary, insurance brokers were having an increasingly hard time getting business.

We came up with the concept of creating a large, personalised board that brokers could hang in their reception area. The size of a poster, the centre would explain the services offered by the broker and the edges would display advertising from local businesses that customers might find useful, such as solicitors, plumbers and car body repairers. It was aptly named a BusinessBoard.

The idea was that we would provide the boards to insurance brokers for free and receive recurring income from selling the adverts. In turn, brokers would benefit by forging greater links with the advertised firms, who might also recommend them to clients. Additionally, we would leave business cards for the local advertised firms with each broker, so they could hand them out to clients. Our costs were considerably lower than for the directory business, as we had much less printing to do, and yet we still received a similar income, meaning it quickly become a profitable business. That was when my obsession with business models began.

Initially though, we could not find anyone who was interested in getting involved, largely because BusinessBoard was not a compelling name. After consulting a friend who had sold a successful advertising company, we changed the name to Insurance & Legal and sales immediately began to take off.

This same friend introduced me to Peter Grimley, who has been my personal accountant for nearly 25 years; he's as straight as a die, a prerequisite I would recommend in your accountant. In turn, Peter introduced me to John Loebl, the best tax accountant I have ever met, who is similarly as honest. I am enormously grateful to both Peter and John, as they have each given me great business advice and their records have always been meticulous. As a result, I have consistently received a clean bill of health from tax inspections over the years and I can sleep soundly at night.

Besides the name change, we introduced a rolling contract, which meant that advertisers would continue to pay for their adverts to be displayed until they contacted us to ask for them to be removed. This could sometimes take years – the big advantage of calling it Insurance & Legal was that the standing order payments would appear on a bank statement as Insurance, so accounts departments would be reluctant to cancel them in case it was an important insurance contract.

In the early days, we had no money to spare and were keen on saving a few pounds wherever we could. Our efforts to save money on accommodation, however, didn't always work out. For example, my brother and I would sometimes find ourselves spending the night in family homes, sleeping in the rented-out rooms of children who were away at university. We would watch television with the dad in the lounge and in the morning the mum would make us breakfast. In one house we were offered a cup of tea, only to be told proudly that they hadn't cleaned the teapot of its used tea leaves in 30 years and so could make a pot of tea just by pouring water into it. It tasted quite nice, nevertheless.

Once, in Guildford, we accidently ended up spending the night in a YMCA hostel. I had only popped in to ask for directions to the Y Hotel, which we had booked into, but the man at the reception desk asked for my name and told me that we were staying there for two nights. It turned out that the YMCA had spare rooms and had added the name the Y Hotel, which I had to admire. The man at the reception also asked if I had brought any trainers with me, because there was a game of basketball taking place that night and he wondered if I'd like to join in. Sadly I hadn't, but ever since I have travelled with a gym kit and trainers, just in case.

When Nigel turned up, he was not at all impressed by the communal showers and the discovery that we had to carry out a task at breakfast. But we soon saw the funny side and I scraped the plates whilst Nigel loaded them into the dishwasher. We looked slightly out of place wearing suits in a YMCA, but no one mentioned it, and the following night we ended up having a great time in the bar there with the other guests. We did have to go to bed early though, as they turned the lights out at 10.30pm.

Another time, I arrived at a hotel in Reading to find the owner standing behind the reception desk wearing his dressing gown. It did not bode well, but we hadn't been able to find anywhere else to stay nearby so I checked in and headed up to my room. Normally when I arrive at a hotel room, I take my jacket and shoes off, lie on the bed and put the TV on while I wait for Nigel. But this hotel room was so horrible that I didn't even want to go near the bed, never mind lie on it. I knew there was no way that Nigel would like the room either.

A few minutes later, Nigel knocked on the door. When I opened it, he simply announced: "Come on, we're leaving." I said: "Hang on, you haven't even seen the room yet!" He replied: "I know, but a rat has just run past me in the corridor."

We went back down to reception to demand a refund from the owner because we'd seen a rat. He paused a moment and said: "Are you sure it wasn't a cat?" I told him that I thought I could tell the difference between a rat and a cat, so he reluctantly gave us our money back and we left.

Fortunately, we started to make decent money from the business and began to stay in Travelodges. Our success was helped by my introducing a weekly incentive scheme, which meant we were paid in direct proportion to the amount of adverts we had individually sold. Nigel didn't like the idea initially, but I realised that I worked better this way and definitely sold more as a result. I used the money earnt to pay off debts still hanging over me from Prestige.

Running the business was very straightforward. Whenever an advertiser decided to remove their advert, we simply signed up a new advertiser and stuck their advert over the old one. Once we had a couple of hundred brokers signed up, repeat fees from advertisers meant that money would come in each month. We did have to keep going to brokers to replenish the business cards, but at least that was a sign the system was proving useful to them.

I did have one close shave though: I was about to fix a board to the wall of a broker's office and suddenly realised I was going to drill straight into a box of electrical cables. That would have been the end of me! I spent the rest of the day feeling sick, contemplating life and wondering what could have happened. I resolved to be more careful in the future.

Our employees also provided us with the occasional challenge. In one instance, a sales guy, who had been out selling with Nigel, invited Nigel to meet his wife. Just before they entered the house, though, the salesman warned Nigel that his wife might be cross with him. Nigel was confused because he was one of our best-paid salespeople and was making a lot of money for his family.

When Nigel asked why, the guy explained that his wife was angry because he had worked on Christmas and Boxing Day, only spending New Year's Eve with the family. Nigel frowned and said, "But you didn't work for us on those days." The sales guy replied, "Just humour me and don't say anything."

When they walked into the kitchen, the sales guy introduced Nigel to his wife, who was in the middle of cooking dinner; she immediately turned around and threw a full plate of food at Nigel. Fortunately, it missed him and smashed into the wall behind him, the food slowly sliding down the wall.

Nigel was completely baffled but, as he was hustled out of the house, the salesman explained that he actually had a dual life, with two wives and two sets of children living in two different houses. Each wife thought that he was only earning half what he was really earning and both thought that his boss was really mean to make him work every Christmas; in reality, the salesman was simply juggling his time and spending every other year with each family.

He didn't work for us for long after that.

Insurance & Legal Services ran for several years and was an extremely profitable business. My brother and I were making £50,000 each a year, meaning that I could move from a two-bedroom flat to a four-bedroom house. Eventually we realised that we were in a declining market, with the number of brokers falling due to direct competition with the big insurers, but even when we stopped actively running it, the business continued to bring in money for several years – proving the usefulness of recurring income.

My GOLDEN RULES for selling

Under-promise to over-deliver

In a high-pressured situation with a customer, colleague or bank, it's easy to over-promise and under-deliver; to think, 'It'll be all right – I'll make it work', when, in your heart of hearts, you know you're heading for a fall. It's a horrible feeling and can result in all kinds of bad experiences. One trick I devised was to regard meetings like an auction or trip to the casino. If you don't want to lose your shirt, decide on a limit *before* you go in and **write it down**. Even if you scribble it on a scrap of paper as you're walking through the door, the mere act of defining the outer limit of what you can promise will deter you from passing that point. By only promising what you can achieve, you will reap the rewards when you deliver.

The second time you use this trick, try writing down less than you know you can comfortably achieve – you will under-promise and over-deliver, to the delight of all concerned... especially yourself.

Explain the benefit of the benefit of the benefit of the benefit...

It is easy to fall into the trap of explaining the features, rather than benefits of a particular product. 'This DVD player has Dolby sound' means nothing. 'The Dolby sound on this DVD makes you feel like you're at the cinema' is much better. And going deeper works even better: 'because it feels like you're at the cinema, you'll want to watch DVDs at home. As this will cost less than going to the cinema, the DVD player will soon pay for itself.' The benefit of the benefit is persuasive.

Remember their name

Remembering someone's name is profitable.

If you bump into someone you met ages ago and they remember your name but you don't remember theirs, they gain the upper hand simply through you demonstrating that they weren't important to you. If they then ask you to call them about your product or service, you will have to sheepishly ask their name, which really doesn't give a great impression.

But if you remember their name, you'll be more confident and they will be flattered and therefore more likely to do business. It's that simple. Here's how to do it. When you're introduced to somebody, immediately use their name – even if it sounds a bit obvious. It's better that you sound obvious and can still remember that person's name an hour or even a year later, than look cool and forget it.

Another trick is to picture the person standing next to everybody you know with the same name. Huddled together, visualise all the 'Alans' or 'Deborahs' in one group. This is a powerful image, which tends to come back to you.

Lastly, if you can't remember somebody's name, you could say, "I'm terribly sorry, I can't remember your name" and then respond with, "Oh, I knew that, I meant your last name", when they tell you their first name. Although this feels slightly fake to me, it might get you out of an embarrassing spot.

Keep quiet about the competition

Every time you mention a competitor by name, you advertise them. When we were setting up Cardpoint and looking for a processor, businesses would often tell us not to deal with a specific business – of course, we would then promptly phone the business mentioned to find out why. Doing this actually led us to the company that we ended up dealing with.

Find the sticking point

When you are trying to sell something, always ignore the first objection given by the potential buyer – it will not be the real reason. Instead, try to close the deal early, before the buyer is ready to say yes, so they will tell you the real obstacle standing in their way. Then you can address the issue and sort it out.

Add hooks

If you are selling to a large organisation, have lots of hooks in it. You need to ensure that someone in accounts gels with you, that a production team member hits it off with their counterpart, that your salespeople are working closely with their buyers and that you are enjoying regular meetings with the managing director or owner.

Damn with faint praise

If asked about a competitor, you should always use this technique. If somebody says, "What do you think about XYZ Company", you should say, "I don't think they are as bad as other people say they are" and then say nothing else. It works a treat, you don't look disingenuous nor have you foolishly advertised the competition by saying "They're OK".

Make time for face time

The more often you see your existing customers, the more you will sell to them. It's doubly beneficial to see existing customers as often as you can, as they are the easiest to sell more things to.

Going Postal

I was trying to think of a new business idea when Yellow Pages called to ask what section I would like to list our business phone number in. Back then, if you had a business phone line, they would give you a free listing in their directory.

On a whim, I told them to list it under Private Detectives.

Two weeks after the new *Yellow Pages* directory was delivered, I received a call from a woman wanting to hire me to follow her husband because she suspected he was having an affair. We agreed on £150 for my services and she told me that her husband worked at British Aerospace and drove a Rover.

Now, at the time, British Aerospace had just bought Rover, so almost all of its employees had taken advantage of a staff deal and bought one. When I parked outside the British Aerospace car park, almost every car was a Rover; they all looked exactly the same and, worse still, they all had similar number plates. I quickly started to go a bit mad trying to find the correct car.

Eventually the husband emerged from the car park in his Rover, so I followed him at a discreet distance to a nuclear processing site a few miles away. His wife had told me that he might go there, as he was a member of their social club's squash club. I watched him park his car and go in and then I parked myself and settled down to wait.

Unfortunately, a nuclear waste processing site isn't the sort of place where you can just loiter. Within minutes a car had pulled up next to me and four burly security guards got out and surrounded the car. One of them knocked on the window and asked if he could help me. I said: "It's alright, I'm just parked." He said: "Well you aren't parking here, mate, this is a secure site and if you don't leave right now, we'll call the police."

This was not going well. I said: "Well, actually I am a private detective and I'm trying to catch this guy who is supposed to be having an affair."

They clearly didn't believe a word of it and I was not so politely escorted from the premises. When I told the wife I had failed to find out anything about her husband, she wasn't impressed either. That was the end of my career as a private detective – the next time someone called asking for my services I quickly declined.

Nigel and I actually came up with our next business, Postal Facilities Limited, while we were parked at a petrol station in Norwich eating sandwiches. Having done so well out of advertising with Insurance & Legal Services, I realised that outdoor advertising next to the point of sale could be even more successful.

I decided to approach petrol companies about advertising on their forecourts, but they all wanted too much money just to display a poster. I needed to put the advertising onto something useful in order to make it financially viable.

I found out from the petrol companies that their three most requested things were postboxes, the National Lottery and cash machines. So I asked Royal Mail if I could put advertising on their postboxes – an idea they dismissed out of hand. But by then I was inspired by this possible opportunity and decided to investigate whether I could produce my own postbox with advertising on and have the letters collected by Royal Mail.

The solicitors and barristers I approached for advice were useless, so I enrolled at night school to do the first year of a law degree in order to determine if I could have mail collected from my own postbox. I discovered in the Telecommunications Act that private businesses like hotels were allowed to have a postbox, including one not owned by the business itself. There were some requirements – you needed to have a certain type of lock and pay a Royal Mail fee – but the discovery was enough for me to realise that I had found my next eureka moment.

We asked a local sheet metal company to make up a postbox from a sketch we'd given them. It cost £300 and was ready for collection two weeks later. Nigel and I went along to collect it and, although I didn't know what we were expecting, we definitely expected something more polished than the metal monstrosity given to us: it looked like a poorly welded Dalek, something which couldn't have looked less like a postbox if it had tried.

Fortunately, when we spray painted it with Hammerite 'Postbox Red' it came to life, but something was still missing. I jogged to the nearest postbox and noticed that there was a black stripe at the bottom, which is apparently put there to stop dust and rainwater from tainting the red paint. We bought some masking tape and sprayed the bottom two inches of the box black. Our postbox was born.

I applied to Royal Mail for a collection and we installed the post box at a petrol station in Kent a few weeks later using full voltage power tools. We later discovered that you shouldn't use these on petrol forecourts, but at the time we had no idea we were breaching regulations – we hadn't even coned the area off. Once installed, Royal Mail came to fit a lock and started collecting from it the following day. After two and a half years of battling, we were in business.

As planned, we began to sell advertising on the side of our postbox. Nigel sold the biggest advert to a fishing tackle shop, which paid £470 upfront. At that point, we realised that putting adverts on a postbox situated on the wall near to the cash tills could be very popular with advertisers.

When I contacted the Royal Mail to ask about the specifications required for further boxes, they told me that I needed an *aperture*. I had no idea what an aperture was, so asked for a break in the meeting to phone my brother and ask him. I shouted down the phone to contact our suppliers, find out if any of them did apertures, how much they were and where we could buy them. Nigel didn't know what an aperture was either, so looked it up in the dictionary. It turned out that an aperture was simply another name for a hole – so much for a private school education.

Whenever I secured a meeting with a petrol company, I would take a full-sized postbox with me to show them what it looked like. At two-foot tall and wide, made of metal, and weighing at least 40kg, I would carry it with some difficulty in a bag on my back.

One day I arrived at BP's offices in Milton Keynes, drenched in sweat because I had had to park miles away, and wearily put the postbox down on the floor. The women at the reception desk took one look at me and said: "Gosh, you look a bit flustered." I laughed and said: "Yes, in my next life I'm going to be a laptop salesman. They will be an awful lot easier to carry around."

We installed five more postboxes and Nestlé paid to put an advert on the side of them. It was called 'The Best Break' and featured Nescafé coffee and KitKat. One of our postboxes was installed at a BP petrol station in London and at 4pm the same day the owner rang us. I was not sure whether to take the call because I thought he may be unhappy for some reason. However, the owner was delighted because he had sold out of Nescafé and KitKats and had had to send his brother to the cash-and-carry supermarket to buy more. The strength of the response generated by displaying the advert so prominently by the door of his petrol station was staggering.

We had been funding the postbox business with money made from Insurance & Legal, but by the time we had installed six boxes we had run out of money to further invest. However, we had secured an outline agreement from Nestlé to advertise on a further 1,000 postboxes at a rate of £1,000 per box per year, so, in 1999, we were able to sell the business to the advertising company More O'Ferrell Adshel on the basis of the future revenue it would generate.

Since we could see so much potential in the business, it was painful to sell, so we asked for a sell-on clause in the sales contract with More O'Ferrell Adshel. This meant that we would be paid a further sum of money if the business was sold on. This is sometimes called an anti-embarrassment clause if a big company sells an asset under value and the new owner quickly sells it again for a large gain. We believed that, as the postboxes were rolled out, postal administrations across the world would see their strategic value, particularly in light of the liberalisation of the postal market which opened up Royal Mail to competition.

More O'Ferrell Adshel was reluctant to include a sell-on clause, but eventually agreed at 1am on the final night of negotiations. We did the deal the following morning and ended up being paid almost £1m for the business. It was a slam dunk moment which didn't come a moment too soon. I had so little money left that I didn't even have enough in my bank account to pay the £20 fee to fast-track the payment of my bankers' draft. My brother banked with Yorkshire Bank and, as there was no branch in London at that time, he had to sleep with his bankers' draft under his pillow to keep it safe.

More O'Ferrell Adshel kept us on as consultants for two days a week to oversee the expansion of the business. We installed another 1,200 postboxes at virtually every major petrol retailer, with Nestlé advertising on them all. In 1999, after 40 of a 42 months' sell-on clause arrangement, we sold the company on behalf of More O'Ferrell Adshel to none other than Royal Mail. We were duly paid again, this time giving us a payment of several hundred thousand pounds.

This was particularly gratifying to us, as, years earlier, during a heated debate with Royal Mail, with whom we had a rather strained relationship, one of the main directors told me: "Mills, we have been in business for 300 years, we don't need the likes of you." He now had to sanction the acquisition of my company to avoid it falling into the hands of the German or Dutch Post Offices, which had both shown serious interest in buying it.

With the money received from the sale, we decided to look at investing in London property. On further investigation though, we decided the £100,000 price tag for a three-bedroomed flat in Kensington was as high as it was going to go, so didn't buy it. That same flat would now be worth many millions of pounds: not one of our best decisions.

With our new-found wealth and unemployed status, Nigel and I decided to go to New York and look for a new business idea. We bought the cheapest possible flights and our luggage went astray on the way, so we ended up flying to Washington to retrieve it, but we eventually made it to New York. We would sit in Starbucks every morning and agree that coffee shops would never take off in the UK because we are a nation of tea drinkers. Another great decision.

We looked with interest at the internet cafés in New York as a possible idea for the UK, but decided that the cost of starting up would be too high. One day, we ended up in a convenience store in Manhattan in search of a Diet Coke and saw an internal cash machine, something I'd never seen before. I inserted my British Abbey National card into it and it charged me $3 to withdraw $50.

Eureka, I thought. "Nige, we've cracked it," I said.

My GOLDEN RULES for getting started in business

Ditch the perfect set-up

Over the years I've learned that an imperfect set-up which allows you to trade is better than a non-trading, perfect set-up. If you have a great idea for a business and then spend loads of time sourcing premises, ordering stationery, arranging a new car, computer and printer, you'll lose momentum. On the other hand, if you can get started and trade profitably with nothing but your mobile phone and your clapped-out car, you'll make time later to sort the niceties out.

We sold our postbox business, Postal Facilities, twice whilst it was based in an old Fire Station, and nobody could have cared less. Concentrate on doing the right things, rather than doing things right, so you can start trading and making profits. The rest can wait.

Be all over it

Make it a priority to know everything about your business and how it works. I still meet chief executives who know lots about one bit of their business and have no idea about the rest. To be in a strong position, you have to be all over your business.

Understand that a scalable business is a saleable business

My wife used to envy professionals such as doctors, lawyers, accountants and dentists, as they all seemed to earn good money year in and year out. And yes, some do terrifically well, but how can they scale their income up? If you charge by the hour, consultation or service, you only earn when physically doing a task.

However, the postbox business formula meant that the administration of 50 boxes was pretty much the same as for our eventual 1,200. Therefore, when I found an advertiser, I could sign them up for 1,200 × £1,000 per year even before the postboxes were all installed.

If you have to actually be in your business to generate income – whether it's baking bread, advising a client, treating a patient or driving a vehicle – then you will always be limited by how many hours there are in the day. However, if you can orchestrate others to perform the task simultaneously and many times over, you will generate more income and more profit and, in the process, create a business that someone else might want to buy. Remember, the best builders may never lay a brick, the owner of an airline does not have to know how to fly a plane and the owner of a hotel chain does not have to make up every bed in each hotel.

Harness the value of recurring income

Aim to create a business with recurring or ongoing income. If you can produce something once and sell it many times, or charge per usage, it's highly effective. For example, if you're selling computers, consider offering maintenance contracts to your customers as well as peripherals, such as printers and scanners, and consumables, like paper, toner, and ink. You can then sign customers up to an ongoing monthly contract that brings in a regular income. This is something we lacked at Prestige. If I could have engineered one tenth of a penny of everything spent on phone calls from payphones, or a percentage of the line rentals paid for by our telephone system customers, we would have made a fortune.

Be independent of location

If you start a business which is entirely dependent upon its location, you are exposing yourself to the risk that the location you have chosen will one day become less popular. For example, businesses in seaside towns really suffer when budget airlines start flying holidaymakers to different countries.

If you can develop your business in multiple locations or in a way that can be relocated, better still, if you can operate it virtually so that the location is irrelevant, you'll build a more sustainable, profitable business.

Play nice

You never know when you'll come across somebody again, even in the unlikeliest of circumstances. Business is a long game and remembering this will prevent you from falling out with people.

The Birth of
Cardpoint

After withdrawing $50 from the cash machine in a Manhattan corner store, we ran to the local internet café and began searching for manufacturers and companies which operated cash machines in the US. We found lots of them.

We contacted many of them to see if we could structure a deal to operate machines in the UK and have the transactions processed in the US.

It turned out this wasn't feasible, so we tried to speak to UK processors. This included speaking to UK cash machine governing body LINK, which refused to put me through to anybody and would then cut me off.

The cash machine business model was very simple and easy to explain, a key attribute later on when we needed to raise money for it. I used to explain it in 30 seconds – known as an 'elevator pitch', which all business people should have for their business – like this:

"You insert your card and enter the PIN. You then select how much cash you want: for example, £60. The machine asks if you will accept the charge of £1.50 and, if you say yes, your account is debited £61.50. You receive £60 in nice notes and we receive the £1.50 overnight, giving us no bad debt or debtor days."

It's worth presenting your pitch in the second person, i.e., "if you buy one of our computers, you will benefit from…"

Any time someone describes their business to me this succinctly and with that level of information, I know I've found a successful business person. A short pitch helps you to win customers, explain your requirements to suppliers, recruit staff, raise money and *save time*.

People hate you wasting their time, so if you can keep it brief, do so – and *rehearse* it. I can still say this elevator pitch without even thinking.

We needed a sponsor bank for our cash machine business, so one day I phoned every bank, starting with A through to Z, trying to talk to someone. After many phone calls, I reached a woman at Woolwich who passed me to her boss, Mick McHale, who agreed to act as our sponsor. He was instrumental in enabling us to launch our business.

I was using a lawyer called Frank Shephard from Halliwells, a mid-sized Manchester firm, for our legal negotiations. When the two of us turned up at the offices of Clifford Chance, the law firm representing Woolwich, we discovered that their team consisted of two barristers, four solicitors, seven assistants, three managers and a director. As we entered the room, I thought we'd disturbed a conference until I saw Mick McHale's face.

The two of us were completely outnumbered, but nevertheless managed to strike a very satisfactory deal – not least because we took a bold approach. Just before we walked into the meeting, I told Frank to ask the Woolwich team for a five-year, exclusive agreement to use their logo on the side of our cash machines. Frank said they would never agree, but I said since I was instructing him, he had to ask for it, and with a straight face. He did, and one barrister burst out laughing, while we just sat there with completely deadpan expressions. The barrister asked for a break and, when their team came back in, he accepted a five-year, exclusive agreement. We couldn't believe it.

We learnt a big lesson from that – don't be afraid to ask for something, even if you are the underdog, because sometimes it works and you get what you asked for.

Our first machine went live on 17 March 2000, nine months after we had first seen that cash machine in the United States. The first three machines were installed by my brother and me, including one at the BP garage in London where our postbox was. We initially called the business CashCard, for which I created a simple black and white logo.

When we came up with the idea of installing charging cash machines in the UK, no one had done it before. Yet we did not install the first machine – we were beaten to it by another company, called Euronet, which installed one just a few months before we did. However, we found that it was actually quite useful to have a competitor, because they could go and explain how charging cash machines worked to a potential client and when we visited them they already understood how they operated. For that reason, I have always been relaxed about being a fast follower rather than a pioneer.

Just before we brought the machines into service, we were called by Kevin Beerling, who had worked at More O'Ferrell Adshel (the company that had bought out postbox business). Kevin had been the financial controller there and we had stayed in touch with him after the sale because we had taken part of the payment in loan notes. Loan notes are a way of paying for acquisitions in instalments: you receive an initial payment upfront and then further payments in subsequent years, with interest, which spreads your tax bill. For the seller, it's a way of deferring the cost of the purchase; for the buyer, it gives a better rate of interest than a bank would – as long as you aren't worried about how secure the company paying you is.

Kevin had diligently rung us each year, two or three weeks before the loan repayment was due, to give us the interest calculation and despatch the cheques. He eventually left to become finance director of Ambient, who owned the subsidiary Moneybox – a rival charging cash machine company who started operating at the same time as us and Euronet. At a board meeting it was mentioned that two brothers were starting up a cash machine business and Kevin realised that it was us. When he explained to the CEO that he knew us, he was told to get in contact.

I met Kevin for a drink and he raised the idea of us not launching our business and instead collaborating with Moneybox. Although we were flattered by the approach, we knew we could make more profit by remaining independent. And we were right. Five years later it was us who acquired Moneybox, not the other way round.

Kevin later told me he had warned Moneybox that they would need to be careful of us as competitors because he had seen Nigel and me in action. But they had laughed off his warning, saying, "We don't need to worry about two guys from Blackpool." Little did they know.

My GOLDEN RULES for communicating

The worst thing always comes last

If someone wants something from you, to tell you something unpleasant or chastise you, I have invariably found that they will do it at the end of the conversation. You can spend whole meetings talking about anything and everything, until you are confronted with the one topic you are there to discuss.

With a supplier, it may be that they want to tell you about a price rise or a stock shortage. With staff, it's normally about a pay rise, a co-worker problem, a need for a loan or a grievance. With family, it's about the frequency of your visits, an interaction you had or your future plans. With lots of people, it's about money.

These kinds of meetings can be frustrating, because you want your supplier to just get to the point about the price increase they are evidently going to serve you with. However, if you know what is coming – and I usually have a pretty good idea – then you can use the first 55 minutes to position yourself and possibly dilute the confrontation – or even disarm the coming argument. Don't try to eke the issue out of them. Use the time to your advantage, so you have a bigger chance of winning when they finally reach the contentious bit.

You may even find this delaying tactic useful yourself – just make sure to leave yourself enough time, as there's little point in frittering 55 minutes of a scheduled hour session away only to then raise an issue that requires constructive debate, detailed agreement and an action plan.

Sometimes I even flip this. If you have something difficult that you need to talk about, everyone expects you to do loads of preamble. Instead, I go straight in with the gritty issue, ensuring that other people in the meeting are unable to do any positioning or disarming themselves.

Learn the act of non-verbal communication

To be successful you must project what you are saying both verbally and non-verbally – your body is saying as much as your mouth is, if not more.

You will probably already know that someone folding their arms is a sign they are being defensive or rejecting your opinion, but you don't have to do anything as overt as cross your arms to give a lot away.

However you act, whether you are conservative in your presentation or flamboyant in waving your arms around, such actions will be more effective if they convey your true intentions. At all costs, you want to avoid people thinking that although you *told* them one thing, you actually *meant* another.

Check your terminology

When we first launched our cash machine business, everybody referred to them as '*surcharging*' cash machines. Yet once I thought about this, I realised that, as *sur* is the French word for *on*, it felt like *surcharging* meant a charge on top of another charge. Our cash machines only made one charge, so I taught everyone to drop the *sur* and start calling them *charging* cash machines. This was then refined to become cash machines with a convenience fee. Did it matter, and did we make more money? I'll never know. But it certainly felt better.

You may not be able to spot negative terminology in your business. Ask a friend or family member to discuss your business with you and tell them all of the words a customer hears. There may not be any negative ones, but you may find a few areas where you can improve the description you give, which may differentiate you from your competitors.

Practise and plan

It's important to rehearse before any big presentation. When my wife, Angela, was working and needed to convince her boss to hire a PA to help her, we did a bit of role play with me acting as her boss. We went through the arguments, discussed the benefits, and refined the phrases she would use. When she put the suggestion to her boss the following day, he agreed and thought it was a good idea – despite the increase in his payroll costs.

Ask a friend, relative or colleague to pretend to be the person you're meeting, put on the clothes you intend to wear and act out how you want the meeting to go. Do it in the pub with a drink and it normally turns into a hoot too! When Neil Armstrong stepped onto the moon, he famously said, "that's one small step for man; one giant leap for mankind." But what a lot fewer people know is that his next sentence was: "It's just like we planned it." Plan first to improve your chances of success.

Always expect the best from people...

It was my daughter, at age seven, who taught me this lesson. My children always make loads of friends on holiday – starting with the taxi driver on the way to the airport, the other kids around the swimming pool, the hotel staff and so on. In this instance, when my wife, three children and I flew home from Disney World in Florida, we had to sit in three rows of two seats on the plane. I ended up sitting next to a stranger.

The stranger and I politely chatted about the weather, families, and so on. About an hour into the flight, my daughter Isabella peered round the side of her seat. "Dad! Dad!" she loudly whispered. "What's your new friend called?" Bless her, she'd always heard me ask the names of her new friends, and she'd just assumed I'd made a new friend for life. Children are great at reminding you to look for the good in the world.

Beware the phrase 'with respect'

Over the years, whenever I've heard these words, they have invariably been followed by something disrespectful, usually an insult.

Once, I was having lunch with my accountant and his colleague when the colleague proceeded to get extremely drunk. After the meal, we travelled together to London to attend a dinner celebrating a deal. At one point in the journey, the colleague leaned over to me and slurred: "With respect, you're a chancer."

My accountant tried everything he could to quieten his colleague, but I just laughed. When we reached London, the man was too drunk to eat and was put to bed at 7.30pm. He missed the whole evening and was ill for days afterwards. Funnily enough, I never instructed him again.

Watch out for the words 'with respect' and be careful when you think you are about to say them. Are you about to be disrespectful? And, if so, will it cost you? If not, let it go with both barrels, but don't expect a long-term relationship afterwards. Be very careful.

Floating
Cardpoint

A s the business started to grow, I began to look for simple ways to increase our customers' attachment to us and help them feel we were on their side.

When we switched to an automated phone system, for example, everyone started complaining about it. In response, I decided to secure a memorable phone number and put it on all the cash machines, so at least customers would be able to contact us easily. I felt that if we could encourage our customers to ring us when there was a problem, we would probably sell them more machines because we could talk to them and begin a personal relationship – something which can be difficult when you have 1,000 machines.

I managed to acquire the number 0845 222 2222 for £5,000, so we put it on every machine. We started getting calls from people saying they would like one of our machines in their shop but had been unable to remember our number until then. Having a memorable phone number even helped improve our retention rate. For example, I spoke to the owner of a Spar shop and he told me, "The thing is Mark, your machine is a bit hopeless, as it's always going wrong. But I had a vote with the staff and they said that since we can all remember your phone number, we might as well carry on with you." And he renewed his contract.

By the time the business had been running for a year, we had installed 37 cash machines and I felt we had a strong story to tell investors about our potential for growth. We also knew that we were not going to have enough money to fund this growth ourselves so, at the end of 2000, I contacted a broker to discuss the idea of floating the business on the Alternative Investment Market (AIM) in London.

As a general rule, the best way to fund your business is to find the money you need from cashflow. Second to that is to borrow money, whether from friends, family or the bank – provided you can repay them. If you cannot do any of these, you need to sell equity. We had exhausted the first two options, so floating our business on AIM was the obvious next step. Not only would this give us funding straightaway, and generate publicity, but the move would provide us with a structure able to raise more money in the future, as we could simply sell off shares in the business.

But after several meetings with the brokers, I received a phone call from one of them as I was driving away, saying that he didn't think it was a good idea to float the business at this point. They felt that it was too early. Although the business was doing well, it had only been trading for a year and still had relatively few cash machines in operation. Also, we hadn't yet positioned the business in the market to properly show off its future potential.

I wasn't willing to give up on floating the business, however, as we could see massive potential in the idea. Yet we had already invested all the money made from our previous ventures into it, so couldn't grow it further without a big injection of capital to enable us to move up a gear. In a bid to work out which brokers were floating companies of our size and in our type of industry, and therefore might be interested in floating us, I started studying the *Financial Times*. The broker name Beeson Gregory kept popping up, so I contacted them and we started having monthly meetings to discuss the idea.

During this time, I started to better position the business for a float. First to go was the name. At this point the business was still called CashCard, a name I felt was far too limiting for the kind of services our machines could potentially offer in the future. Although our machines only dispensed cash, they were effectively small, secure electronic authorisation terminals which could be used in other ways, such as topping up pay-as-you-go mobile phones. We spent a lot of time trying to think up a better name, without the word cash in it, and eventually our accountant, Peter Dawson, came up with the name Cardpoint.

I also began to set up the business in the way a publicly listed company would be expected to operate. We decided, for example, that we would not lease photocopiers or company cars, because these things complicated the accounts and made it hard to see how well the business was trading.

The following Christmas I met with Henry Turcan, Mike Brennan and Christian Hobart, from the broker firm, who said they liked the idea of floating our business. On the way back to their offices I told them I had a piece of paper in my car I wanted to show them, so we all walked to my car to fetch it. I had just bought myself a new BMW Series 5, which cost me £55,000, and when they saw the car I could tell they realised I was a credible person, who wasn't just looking to float the business for a quick buck. By the end of the month, they confirmed they were happy to handle the float for us. I am not sure that if I had still been driving my old estate car they would have made the same decision.

Over the next few months, my new financial director, Chris Hanson, and I wrote a marketing presentation and embarked on a roadshow to investors to drum up interest in our float. We also agreed a debt facility with the Bank of Scotland for £3.5m, which was granted on the condition that we raised another £2.5m in equity through the flotation.

At one roadshow, a City institution investor asked how much the business would be valued at. Our broker looked at his feet, coughed, ummed and ahhed and generally avoided the question. I kicked him under the table and said £6m. When the investor asked how I'd arrived at that figure, I said, "It's fair to me, fair to you and is a reasonable mid-point." The investor accepted my argument and during the next 30 or so presentations, most other investors did too. Some said it was too high, but that's all part of the game.

However, at one presentation when I mentioned the figure of £6m an investor replied, "We'll decide the valuation, not you!" I politely pointed out that it was still my company in its entirety and, with the greatest respect, only I could determine its worth and so only I would decide its valuation.

He swore at me...

I said, "You won't be investing then..." and we left, laughing all the way to the car. I may have been seen as arrogant, but I knew that the business was strong and that investors would make money from it.

Despite that investor's sniffy attitude, the flotation did value the business at £6m, and we raised £6m: £2.5m in equity from selling shares and £3.5m in bank debt. Our investors were made up of some very established City institutional investors, with one investor even offering to buy up all the shares ahead of the flotation if we had wanted to take this route.

Neither I nor Nigel took any money out of the business for ourselves at this point, something we felt sent an important message of commitment to the other shareholders. In fact, we actually put more money in. A week before the flotation I told my wife Angela that I had put every penny of our savings into the float. She laughed and said, "The problem with you, Mark, is that you are no good with money in the bank; you always need to bet your shirt and have the thrill of getting down to nothing and living on your wits." The week before the float my blood pressure was probably through the roof, because the business had no more money and I had no more money to put into it – so the float absolutely had to happen. I was greatly relieved when it did. I ended up being the biggest shareholder in the company, with a 35% stake, while Nigel had a slightly smaller stake.

I did make one mistake. Before the float, I met two entrepreneurs who were starting up businesses themselves and we all agreed to invest £20,000 into each other's businesses, in return for a 10% stake. They had an absolute bonanza with Cardpoint, turning their £20,000 into £1m, but I lost the £40,000 I had invested because both their businesses failed. I think once they realised that Cardpoint was such a winner they completely took their eye off their own businesses.

Unfortunately, this diluted my stake in Cardpoint. Yet, the reality is you are better off with a 10% stake worth £1m, then a 50% stake worth £100,000. People become obsessed with hanging onto as big a percentage of their business as possible, but this actually can inhibit you. Your control over your business is determined by your capability: I knew my business better than anyone because I lived and breathed it. I was in 6.5 days a week and so, to me, it didn't matter if I had no stake at all, I knew that I was the best man for the job.

The £2.5m in equity we were raising equalled a flotation price of 43p a share, the price that the shares are initially listed on the stock market. Our brokers told us that flotations usually took place at a round number, so advised that we float at 40p a share instead. But, in my youthful arrogance, I insisted on floating at 43p a share. This turned out to be a mistake.

On the day of the float, the price dropped to 40p. The brokers said,

"That's because it should have been 40p in the first place, the market has taught you a lesson." They were right, of course, the market ultimately decides the price. We would have been better off floating at the slightly lower price of 40p and then perhaps seeing it rise to 47p.

The other mistake I made was over the stock market ticker. Every company which lists on the stock exchange is given a market ticker for its shares, which brokers use to identify stock when they are buying and selling it. Ours was supposed to be CRPT, an abbreviation of the word Cardpoint, but I objected to that because I thought it looked like the word 'crapped'. I asked our brokers if we could have the letters CASH instead. It turned out we could, but it would take time to change from one ticker to the other. On the day of the flotation, no one could buy shares because we'd told people that the marker was CASH when the shares were actually still listed under CRPT. It was only changed to CASH the following day. So that didn't help the share price either.

There was one small upside to this whole fiasco. Whenever I was subsequently interviewed by journalists, I would tell them that our stock market ticker was CASH and joke that if there was ever a stock market crash, someone might phone their broker and tell them to sell everything and put it all into *cash*. This would invariably be included at the end of their article, giving us loads of publicity.

With the £6m raised, we were able to increase the amount of cash machines we had from 188 to 300. It was quite an emotional moment when we reached 300 machines. It was 9pm on the last day of the financial year and everyone was still in the office because we were waiting for Alastair, one of our managers, to complete the installation of the 300th machine in Brighton.

He rang the speakerphone in the office and said, "If this machine gives me £10 now, we are at 300 machines." He tapped in his PIN, the machine gave him the money and everyone cheered. One of my employees even burst into tears. It was a great end to the year.

There were downsides to having external shareholders though. One shareholder was an aggressive hedge fund, who used to do incredibly detailed analysis of our company's financial data. This could sometimes be useful, even if the advice they tried to give us could be rather strange. One time, they calculated that we should increase the fee for withdrawing cash to £2.43 and couldn't understand that, while this might be a great idea financially, it really wasn't going to go down well with our customers.

Another day, I was holding a board meeting when Diana Harris, my PA, came into the room looking rather flustered. She told me that the guy from the hedge fund was on the phone, demanding to speak to me. I said that I would call him back after the meeting but a few minutes later she returned, looking even more flustered, saying that he was refusing to get off the phone until I came out to speak to him.

I told her to hang up on him if she needed to, but that I wasn't interrupting my meeting.

When I called him back afterwards and asked how I could help, he said: "Well first of all, I want you to sack your PA." I told him that I wasn't going to sack my PA and asked why I would do that. He replied: "Because I am a shareholder and I'm going to wait on the line until you have sacked her because she wouldn't put me through to you."

I reminded him that although he owned shares in my company, he didn't own my PA and he certainly didn't own *me*, so I wasn't sacking anybody. We had a pretty fierce conversation and funnily enough we weren't the best of friends after that.

My GOLDEN RULES for building a strong team

Adopt the FARMS approach

At Cardpoint I figured out that people work for five main reasons: Fun, Achievement, Recognition, to Meet the boss and for a Salary (FARMS). If you can introduce these elements into your business, then your employees will be hugely loyal.

The first reason people go to work is because it's **fun**. You could be paying an employee really well, but if they aren't having fun, they will still go to work elsewhere for less money because they think it will be more enjoyable.

As the boss, you have to consciously think about how you are going to create a fun workplace. It's no good saying it's fun here and just assuming employees are going to have a great time at their desk. You need to actively think about what you can do as a company to make a difference and work at it.

We used to organise a really big Christmas party every year. We would take over the Hilton hotel in Blackpool, invite everyone who worked for Cardpoint and their partners, and pay for everything – including an overnight stay at the hotel (even though most people lived in Blackpool).

I realised that people would talk about the Christmas party for three months before it and then for three months after it, recounting the night's events. To bridge the gap, I invented the annual Summer Christmas Party, with a barbecue in the garden of a local hotel, which they would also talk about for three months before and after. That way, people would literally be talking about our parties for 12 months of the year and it always felt as though there was something to look forward to. It created huge amounts of goodwill.

We also organised an annual trip to the theme park Alton Towers, hiring a coach and paying for tickets and food. These events helped us immeasurably when we recruited, negotiated and traded, and, most importantly, they made people proud to work for the company.

The second reason people come to work is for **achievement**. People need to feel that they are genuinely achieving something worthwhile with the work they do. If someone's job is to process documents but they never find out why the documents need to be processed, or even what they are used for, that can be really frustrating and demoralising.

Employees also need to have **recognition** for their achievements, with occasional thank yous and notes of appreciation. If you thank someone in front of everyone in the office, that will mean a lot to them. Even when the pressure is on at work, I always make a point of saying thank you to people and remembering to send birthday cards and flowers, because I know that people appreciate it and that it really does make a difference to their feeling of well-being.

People also need to **meet the boss** – no matter how fleeting the encounter. If someone works for Virgin, for example, people ask them whether they have met Richard Branson. If they have been working there for ten years and haven't met him, they are going to feel pretty silly. So Richard Branson is very good about organising big events where he shakes hands with thousands of employees so that they can tell people they've met him at a party and knows who they are. It stops them feeling as though they work for a faceless organisation.

Lastly, you obviously need to pay your employees a **salary**. In reality though, money is the least important motivator, as all the other elements count far more in terms of job satisfaction.

FARMS seemed to really work, as a few people who worked at Cardpoint even got married to each other, which really pleased me.

Beware the CV enhancer

If anybody says or even implies that they want to work for you to enhance their CV, you should never employ them. The only people I employ are enthusiastic at the interview and seem genuine about the company's product and service. When we interviewed people for jobs at Cardpoint, for example, I was astounded by the number of candidates who proudly told me that they had never used one of our machines and never would.

Now, you could say that these were just very organised people, who had the good sense to avoid paying a fee to withdraw money – an act which fell into the category of using a luxury item – however, if I gave them a job they might well have the wrong mindset. When interacting with a customer, they may be thinking, 'Well, I've never needed to use one, so this person must be lazy and disorganised', when nothing could be further from the truth. In fact, we found that our users saw the fee we charged as good value for money, considering the time and effort it would have taken them to find an alternative.

People who did not and, more importantly, *would not* use our cash machines were clearly not believers in our business, so I would never employ them. I liked employees who said, "Oh, I always use them, it saves time since I can just use the nearest machine." I've always found believers to make the best employees.

Beware past glories

Watch out for potential employees who once had a great job that has dominated their thinking ever since. The kind of people who say, "Oh, when I worked at such and such, those were the glory days…" This is because your business may never inspire that same passion and your employee will constantly be disappointed in your workplace, which will be reflected in their attitude. I've always preferred people who have loved and hated a few places they've worked at because it gives them a more realistic outlook and approach to their working life.

Employ hungry salespeople

For many years, when asked what I did for a living, I would reply "salesman". Normally, the enquirer would then say "Oh, and what do you sell?" To which I would reply, "Well, what do you want to buy?" It served as an ice-breaker but there was a serious point to it as well, as I've never understood why the occupation of salesperson is not more highly regarded.

If you employ salespeople, they tend to fall into two categories. One type, the 1%, focus on selling to customers, championing the cause, evangelising about the product or service, racing around the country closing deals and bringing in orders. The other 99% make up the second type, who spend most of their time talking to colleagues, whinging about expenses and out-of-date product, and complaining about how hard it is out there given the economy, competition or day of the week.

The 99% give themselves away in a very subtle but noticeable way. They basically spend their time selling to you, the boss, rather than to any customers: they will give you presentations, produce reports and statistics, and make you feel that it's your fault that it's so tough 'out there'. They will spend all of their time convincing you of their benefit to the company, and worst of all, they'll try to 'close' you and secure your 'agreement' to keep employing them from one month to the next.

If you have trouble spotting this, and I've been duped countless times, always thinking 'Yes, I know all that but John/Julie is different...', there is one question you need to ask which will embarrass them into either selling or resigning. That question is this: "*Specifically*, what reasons have your customers given you for not buying *this week*?"

If they have seen a customer, they will give you definite answers, such as, "he's not ready until next year", "it won't do X and Y and he needs that as well", or "she says she can only afford £500." While they are talking, take notes – write down the customer names and what they were supposed to have said. The following week, call the salespeople up and again ask them the *specific* reasons customers have given that week.

It only takes a week or two for you to start hearing the same generic Mrs Brown and Mr Smith names and general objections, like "it was too dear", "no one was ready" or "he'd already bought one", as your salespeople won't want to lie in too much detail because it's hard to remember. Keep your notes and specifics and, if need be, ask for the telephone numbers of customers so that you can follow the process up. At this point the salespeople tend to become nervous and may even accuse you of interrogating them, not trusting them and being too full-on, when, after all, they have a job to do. Normally, the salespeople in the 99% category will find another role and leave anyway, blaming you.

Either way, you will soon have enough evidence to prove that they aren't making the requisite amount of calls to make sales or are just fabricating the truth, both dismissible offences.

Lead by example

If you want your team to act in a certain way, you must act that way yourself. Your team members will either conform or you will suggest they find alternative employment.

This behaviour replication is a powerful tool, though, and comes with a warning: your team will do what you do. This includes fiddle their expenses, take 75 minutes for lunch and turn up late to meetings, if that's what you do. To an extent, you are the parent and your team becomes the child.

The positive side of behaviour replication is that if you are honest with your expenses, are prompt, punctual and attentive, then your team will replicate these attributes. If they don't, they are inappropriate for your business and you should act accordingly.

However, sustaining this behaviour requires effort. You may find, for example, that honesty in compiling your expenses comes easily, but you will be tempted from time to time to take longer than you have allowed your team for lunch. Perhaps you are with an important potential client or feel that you need to spend longer with a supplier. Life dictates that there will always be exceptions, but they should remain exceptions. Such instances should only occur when it would do more harm than good to stick rigidly to the behaviour pattern you expect of your team. But whilst an exceptional circumstance regarding a prolonged lunch is occasionally acceptable, any matter related to honesty is **never** subject to exceptional alterations.

Basically, never do anything yourself that you would sack somebody else for. This will make you a good leader.

Accept that success has many fathers

There is an old saying that 'success has many fathers, but failure is an orphan'.

Many people genuinely believe that none of my businesses would have succeeded without them. And, to be fair, without a lot of those people, the businesses would not have fared so well. You will often hear people say they're so important that the company they work for would collapse around the owner's ears if they didn't turn up.

I love it when people think this way, as it creates devotion and loyalty. Let them believe their own importance – it makes for a better workforce if you encourage it by recognising them and rewarding them. Remember, most people work for fun, recognition, time with the boss and then salary, **in that order**. So publicly praise those who achieve for you and generously spread the word that your business's success is attributable to them. At the end of the day, you know what you have achieved.

Understand too that recognition comes in two forms. From your employees' perspective, it is vitally important that you, the boss, recognise their achievements or they'll feel cheated. But, just as importantly, they need to be recognised by their peers and colleagues. I've always found that standing in front of the team and specifically thanking one, two or a group of people for a specific achievement is very motivational.

But equally, don't allow it to annoy you when something goes wrong and nobody wants to be associated with it. Nobody will ever want to own up to failure, as the second part of the saying confirms.

I once read that the characteristic most desired in a leader, whether of a company or a country, is humility. Nobody likes a show-off and if you are genuine when you thank people for the business's achievements, whilst downplaying your own contribution, it will always be warmly received.

You are also allowed, in quiet moments, to pat yourself on the back. After all, no matter how great your team, there wouldn't be a team without you.

On the Acquisition Trail

In the very early days of Cardpoint I was told by a supplier that a small competitor, owned by its Australian parent company, was up for sale. I immediately contacted the CEO and arranged a meeting.

When I arrived at the offices of Direct Cash, they were literally moving out and closing the doors. The CEO and I agreed there and then that I'd buy the assets, stock and signage for £60,000. This basically amounted to some cash machines, some branding accessories and their phone number. The number was particularly useful to us, since they had people ringing up to enquire about their machines, trying to make orders which Direct Cash couldn't fulfil.

The CEO woke up his bosses in Australia to obtain agreement and then we wrote out the key terms of the agreement on a piece of A4 paper. We gave this to a secretary to type, but the computers had already been taken away and the only piece of equipment left was the photocopier. Instead we both signed the handwritten agreement, which the secretary witnessed, and kept a copy each. Then I handed over a cheque for £60,000.

As I was leaving, the CEO gave me a boxful of stickers and some headed paper. On the train home, I struck up a conversation with the man sitting opposite me. When I showed him exactly what I'd bought for £60,000, I had to laugh at the look on his face. It really didn't look like much.

Strategically though, this move gave us more customers, a different telephone number, some new machines and alternative supplier arrangements. I also referred to it as the acquisition of a competitor, marking us out from the crowd as the first cash machine business to embark upon an acquisition trail or which sought to consolidate the industry. These were slightly haughty phrases, but they gave us additional credibility and made everyone take more notice of a young company that was clearly already demonstrating its ambitions.

The Green Machine acquisition was of a more substantial size. Before we floated Cardpoint on AIM, I had met with the two executive directors of Green Machine, a cash machine company based in Brighton. The directors told me that they either wanted to acquire similar businesses or sell their business, since their Irish backer, the billionaire Dermot Desmond, had lost money on his investment and wanted a resolution.

I suggested that, subject to certain conditions, we might like to buy their business, but that I only wanted to engage in the process once we'd done the float. After we completed the float I got back in touch and we began to discuss a deal. I was worried that dealing with Dermot would be difficult, as he was known for being a tough negotiator, so we were all wary. However, although the negotiations took some time, we felt that the team on the other side were honest guys, simply there to do a job and maximise their return.

I was particularly keen to buy Green Machine because, after the sale completed, I hoped to acquire the cash machine division of Securicor. My theory was that Securicor would only take us seriously if we had already made a small acquisition.

When we eventually agreed the deal with Green Machine, one of their team, Jonathan Comerford, told me that Dermot was going to make a loss on his investment at the price they were paying. I suggested that instead of taking cash for the transaction, he take some shares in Cardpoint, which were currently trading at 53p. That way, when the share price reached £1, they would have doubled their money and so wouldn't lose money on the deal. There was no financial benefit to me to suggest that they do the deal this way, I just felt that the best way to do business was to make everyone a winner. The only thing I asked for in return was that when they wanted to sell their shares, they would phone me first; this way, I could arrange for someone to buy them because otherwise it would affect the share price.

The purchase of 105 machines from Green Machine gave us a total of just over 400 machines by October 2002, meaning we had effectively doubled the business in the space of six months.

A couple of years later the share price rose over £1 and Jonathan called me. I'd been expecting his call and had already assembled buyers for his shares, so I just gave him the number of my broker and the transaction proceeded smoothly. I asked Jonathan if I could meet Dermot Desmond in person because I had never met a billionaire before. He agreed and when I was next in Dublin I visited him at his offices.

Dermot was utterly charming and thanked me for helping him turn an investment around. On the way out, I mentioned that I knew he owned the famous Sandy Lane hotel in Barbados. He said that if I ever wanted to go, I should let him know and he would do me a deal – although I should not ask if I could go at Christmas because he couldn't even book his mother in then. When I emailed him, he offered a generous discount on the price, so I have been going every year since. I have an associate who has been going to Sandy Lane for years, paying full price each time, and I couldn't resist showing him the email I had from Dermot. He didn't look very happy.

A few years ago, Dermot was featured in a book and I sent a copy to him, asking him to sign it – he wished me well and added 'the best is yet to come'. No wonder he's a billionaire: great bloke, honest, wise and in six words motivated me for the next ten years.

We raised the money for the Green Machine acquisition by issuing more shares at 53p, which involved spending another week making presentations to investors in the city.

I was somewhat bemused, though, when the headmaster at my children's school congratulated me on the acquisition and said that he was looking forward to dealing with me. We both eventually realised that he thought I had bought the vending machine company that provided fresh fruit for the children, which had the same name, The Green Machine.

By now I had a taste for acquisitions, so having tucked the minuscule Direct Cash under our belt and completed the acquisition of Green Machine, I set my sights higher.

We were a customer of Securicor, the people who transport cash, and our account manager Andrew Martin mentioned that they might be interested in disposing of their cash machine estate. This was a hugely attractive opportunity to me, as I felt that they had a great product which was not being managed to its full potential.

It made perfect sense for Securicor to enter the cash machine market, since they were already doing a great deal of the work involved – buying and installing machines was the logical progression for them. They had also been quite sassy in placing a machine in the newsagents nearest to our offices. I admired that cheekiness, and was a regular user of their machine to check out how it worked, its charges, etc. One day, I noticed they had increased the withdrawal fee from £1, which everybody in the industry was charging, to £1.50.

I immediately increased our charges because I calculated that my loss in usage would be made up for by the huge, in percentage terms, increase in revenue. As it happened, usage remained the same and the sassiness of our competitor installing a machine nearby really had benefited our company (in the epilogue I explain this point in more detail).

Andrew managed to arrange for me to have lunch with their group CEO, Nick Buckles, and I put the idea to him. My proposition was not to just buy Securicor's 1,232 cash machines, but to outsource everything to do with the running and operations of our existing estate back to Securicor at the same time. This would increase Securicor's presence in outsourcing, where they excelled and made good returns, and make the whole deal easier to digest for both parties.

The outlined deal was that we'd pay about £5m upfront and a further £3m in deferred consideration, subject to certain performance criteria. We would raise the money to pay for the acquisition by selling some more equity, which was then trading at 53p a share.

Completing the deal turned out to be a very slow, bureaucratic process, but it was worth persisting because it was a prize we wanted. Fortunately, I had been warned that Securicor could move at glacial speed even when they were keen to progress. In the final stages of drafting the deal, I was holed up with our lawyer, James Sheridan, in our usual hotel, the Hilton on Edgware Road, when we faced a difficult decision. The hotel wanted £1 per page it printed for us and, given the length of the document, our bill would have been thousands of pounds after a day of drafting and re-drafting.

We decided to go for a coffee while we discussed what to do and, while we were walking down the road, we spotted a computer shop. After ten minutes of haggling, we emerged with a printer bought for £89 and a ream of paper. We did more blagging at the hotel, and they gave us another six reams of paper for free. Having a printer of our own saved us a fortune in printing costs and, when the deal was completed, James proudly brought the printer home with us. I've still got it in my office.

There was a big cultural difference between the way that Securicor and Cardpoint operated, which was revealed when we met with Securicor at a hotel near Heathrow. As the morning wore on it started to snow, much to my delight. Although the negotiation was at a critical point, as soon as we broke for lunch I dragged James and our finance director, Chris Hanson, outside. Despite being dressed in suits and ties, we had a massive snowball fight and encouraged other guests to join in. It was a riot and it became even funnier when, during a pincer movement across the car park to try and pin down some other guests who had joined in, we looked up to see the Securicor team sedately lunching and watching us with a look of utter disgust on their faces.

Years later, James asked me to speak at a seminar. During the introduction he told the audience that he'd been asked by clients to do many things, but Mark Mills was the only one who'd ever asked him to "cover me while I cut around that blue Mondeo and ambush the guy in the grey suit."

Meanwhile, we had other issues to deal with. We discovered that our main rival, Moneybox, was trying to persuade our second biggest customer, Granada, who owned motorway service stations, to break their contract so that they could put their cash machines into their outlets instead of ours. I was furious that they would try to do this, so we took out a High Court injunction against both Granada and Moneybox to prevent them from breaking Granada's contract with us. Fortunately, our lawyer Steve Morris and an expert barrister secured injunctions and Moneybox backed off.

As our business grew, we occasionally came up against people – typically journalists or politicians – who would get it completely

KING EDWARD VII SCHOOL

LYTHAM

LANCASHIRE

FY8 IDT

Headmaster: D. Heap, J.P., M.A.
Tel.: 0253 736459

DH/JME

27th May, 1988

Mr. & Mrs. J.F. Mills,
8, Rudyard Place,
St. Annes,
LYTHAM ST. ANNES

Dear Mr. & Mrs. Mills,

I feel that I must inform you officially of an unfortunate incident which happened at school a few days ago.

One of the younger masters, Mr. Fuller, who is also leaving at the end of this term, was thrown in Fairhaven Lake. There were several other boys involved, but Andrew and Mark and their car seem to have been centrally involved.

Presumably, this was intended as some sort of joke. I should be glad of your support in pointing out to Andrew and Mark that it is a joke in very bad taste. It does the School's reputation no good at all; driving cars across ground which is the property of the Local Council to the edge of the lake is illegal; and the master concerned is still limping as a result of the incident. There is no doubt that the matter could be construed as assault if Mr. Fuller wished to pursue it - which fortunately he doesn't.

To be fair to the boys concerned, there have, in the past, been one or two similar incidents but I would have hoped that they would not consider it the sort of tradition that they would wish to continue. Such jokes can have very serious consequences if somebody is hurt. One can envisage circumstances in which this could easily be one of the boys rather than one of the masters.

If any further incidents of this kind were to happen, the point has now been reached where I would feel obliged either to bring an Action in Court on behalf of the member of staff or to exclude any boys involved from taking their exams. here. Though I would find this distasteful and difficult, I am sure you realise that there does come a point when one has to maintain order whatever the cost to individuals concerned. I do hope you will make it clear to Andrew and Mark what my position is.

Yours sincerely,

(*Left*) King Edward VII letter of expulsion, 27 May 1988.

(*Below*) Prestige, circa 1989, outside 'fresh and fruity' shop. From left: Nigel, me and Andrew (three brothers).

(*Left*) Me at Prestige, circa 1989.

(*Above*) Me at Postal Facilities, circa 1997.

(*Left*) Hot air balloon unexpectedly landing in my (big) garden.

(*Above*) The first car I owned at Prestige – very proud of that!

(*Left*) My brother, Nigel, circa 1998.

Forecourts fuel postal concept

BY KATHY LIPARI

TWO former advertising executives will this week launch the first private post operation alongside the Royal Mail in conjunction with the UK's leading petrol retailers.

Over the next five years Postal Facilities will install between 4,000 and 6,000 postboxes on petrol station forecourts.

BP/Mobil, Gulf, Texaco, Elf, The Save Group and Repsol have thrown their weight behind the concept. Mark Mills, Postal Facilities managing director, and his brother, Nigel, have spent the past year in talks with the companies.

The scheme is funded by advertising revenue garnered from companies buying space on a panel on the postbox. Mr Mills said the postboxes would operate in the same way as other Post Office boxes with mail collected and delivered by Royal Mail employees.

Mills: private operation

(*Above*) News clipping from *The Times* Business, 6 April 1998.

(*Left*) Our first
postbox.

(*Right*) Our refined
postbox design.

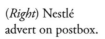

(*Right*) Nestlé
advert on postbox.

(*Left*) Looking for
ideas! Note from the
Marriott hotel in New
York, July 1999.

(*Above*) Friends in high places. Meeting Sir Stelios Haji-Ioannou.

Petrol companies join up to free post box initiative

Postal Facilities is the first company in the UK to offer privately owned post boxes on petrol station forecourts, and has recently installed its 500th post box.

BP, Shell, Texaco, Elf, The Save Group, Repsol, Murco, Fina, Petrol Express, Snax 24 and Jet have all signed agreements with Postal Facilities. A further 3000 post boxes are expected to be installed by the end of this year.

The post boxes are provided free of charge to the petrol stations, with the service being funded by the revenue received from the advertising poster on the front of the post box. The company has recently launched a newly designed post box. The design is unique and easy to recognise, whilst the traditional pillar box red is retained. The addition of the advertising panel allows goods on sale in the store to be promoted at the point of sale.

The post boxes operate in the same way as other Post Office boxes, with mail collected and delivered by Royal Mail employees.

● Tel: 01253 781333

(*Above*) News clipping from *Forecourt*, June 1999.

(*Left*) News clipping from Forecourt, October 1999.

(*Below*) News clipping from *Forecourt*, November 1999.

JAC ROPER'S ADVICE CENTRE

Jac Roper, with more than 20 years' experience in grocery trade journalism, is a recognised expert on problems facing small retailers

MONEY, MONEY, MONEY

What could be handier for customers than a cash withdrawal point just outside the shop – or even inside it. For convenience stores the ATM (automated teller machine) makes perfect sense because their average customer spend is in single figures and therefore likely to be made in cash (see box).

Around £100bn, about one third of all the cash in circulation, is withdrawn annually from the 25,000 plus ATMs in the UK. Although hole in the wall banking has been around for more than 30 years, it is only in recent times that the ATM has found its way into the independent grocery sector.

NatWest claims market leadership in ATMs with 3,300 installed all told, 1,150 of them in 'off-site' locations. But NatWest prefers to do business with chains at head office level as does Bank of Scotland, the other big player which has been very active in the symbol sector.

NatWest will have more than double its

Statistics
● The average cash machine dispenses money to 100 people daily with each person withdrawing £67 on average
● More than three out of five adults now regularly use ATMs via 106 million cards in circulation. APACS predicts that in 10 years' time over three quarters of adults will use ATMs regularly.
● Of the 25,288 UK ATMs, nearly a quarter are sited away from bank branches. These remote ATMs increased by 900 last year to 5,900

Cash is king
According to research carried out on behalf of Girobank – which processes £1 in every £4 passing through UK tills – cash continues to be the nation's first choice in the high street.

The findings showed:
● 85% of payments of £10 are made using cash
● 58% of all payments in supermarkets are made using cash
● 51% of payments in petrol stations are also in cash
● the vast majority of transactions in newsagents, pubs, local grocery stores and on market stalls are in cash

HOLIDAY INCREASE
Employers need to note that from November 23 all workers are entitled to the equivalent of four weeks' paid holiday a year after three months' service (it was previously three weeks pro rata holidays). For example, someone working six hours a week will be entitled to 24 hours paid leave per year.

The regulations under The Working Time Directive apply to all workers including part-timers and anyone over the age of 16. For further guidance ring the DTI helpline on 0845 6000 925.

Mills: brains behind the Advertising Post Box venture

which is probably best described as "a safe with a PC on top" is CashCard Services, operated by Mark Mills who was the brains behind the Advertising Post Box venture.

According to Mills the new business complements the Post Box operation as his long-term plan is to create a 'PostBank' within the convenience sector with parcel transmission, banking, ticket booking and the range of internet support facilities.

Another company already actively engaged in installing internal ATMs is Euronet Services UK. Euronet claims to be the leading deployer of surcharged ATMs with 100 live

number of hole in the wall banks in-stores by the end of this year with some 70 sites installed across six convenience chains. The individual operator is not ruled out but is "not easy" because of the cost of installation" (reckoned to be around £40,000 for each one, including maintenance).

Various criteria must be met, including 24 hour access to the ATM, a certain level of security, the right footfall and turnover. The bank looks for an average of 7,000 transactions per month.

If the big banks are less than keen to deal with independent operators, the gap is being enthusiastically filled by companies happy to install standalone ATMs inside the store. The latest to join this market is a machine

● Tel: 0171 470 1814

Cash in

A new type of convenience cash machine which is simply wheeled into any shop will make the process of withdrawing cash easier and safer for the general public. It offers a new opportunity to retailers to increase customer flow and profit by persuading customers to make the retail outlet their first port of call.

The amount of money withdrawn and spent in the shop covers the rental for the machine and will increase profits significantly. Each Customer using the machine is charged a small amount for the convenience of withdrawing money in a safe well lit place, typically £1 to £2 per withdrawal.

The new business complements Cashcard Services Post Box operation. The long term plan is to create a 'PostBank' within the convenience and forecourt sectors with parcel transmission, banking, ticket booking and internet support facilities. The cash machines also feature on screen advertising which will drive retailer sales.

● Tel: 0181 477 5546

Cashing in on need for ready money

HOW I MADE IT

Mark Mills
founder of
Cardpoint

Money machine: cash dispensers are Mark Mills's fifth business in a career that has encompassed organising parties, a referral system for insurance brokers and phones and postboxes

Rachel Bridge

(*Above*) News clipping from *The Sunday Times*, 11 January 2004.

(*Left*) News clipping from *The Gazette*, 31 December 2007.

A sad closure

ENTREPRENEUR Mark Mills has dubbed the new owners of the business he built up as "old duffers."

It comes after an announcement that Cardpoint is set to close its Blackpool offices following a merger with the loss of around 60 jobs.

But the company was hugely successful under Mark's stewardship, making profits of nearly £20m when he left in September 2006.

No wonder he is sad to see it in its present predicament, particularly since many of the people set to lose their livelihoods will have been his former colleagues at the company's offices on Blackpool Business Park.

(Left) News clippings from *North West Business Insider*, January 2017.

(Below) One of our brighter cash machines!

wrong about how we operated. Against my commercial instincts, we had agreed to install a cash machine in a shop in a little Scottish village which doubled up as a convenience store and a post office. I didn't think that enough people would use it to make it worth our while, but the owners were keen to have a machine because the shop was the hub of the community and the nearest cash machine was 20 miles away. In fact, we always lost money on it, but I kept it there because I felt that we were providing a valuable service for the local community.

One day my wife rang me while I was at work and told me that there was a car parked outside the drive with two people in it, who kept looking at the house. I called the police and one of them came round and knocked on the window of the car. It turned out that they were a journalist and a photographer from the *Sunday Mail.* They eventually emerged from the car and knocked on the door of our house, looking for me. But when my wife asked what the story they were trying to write was, they refused to tell her. She sent them round to my office and later told me that she wondered if I was having a secret affair that was about to be exposed.

When the journalist and photographer arrived at my office, the journalist told me that she was going to write a massive story about how I was exploiting the residents of the Scottish village by charging them £1.50 to make a cash withdrawal. I said fine, go ahead, I will happily take out the machine because it is costing me money. And in its place, I will put your article in a frame on the wall saying that the *Sunday Mail* ran a campaign to have the machine removed. I told the journalist that the villagers were really grateful to have the machine and that if it was taken away they would have to drive to the supermarket 20 miles away instead. The shop would also lose out on all the sales it currently made to people who came in to withdraw cash from our machine – it might even be forced to close. But sure, I said, do go ahead and write your story.

The journalist looked really shocked and ended up writing a tiny piece that was hidden away in the back of the newspaper with a picture of our house. My wife was pretty pleased that it turned out I wasn't having a secret affair too.

The only annoying thing was the *Sunday Mail* article said that I lived in a £1m house, but when we came to sell it, the estate agent was insistent that it was only worth £400,000. I waved the article at him as proof, but he just laughed.

My GOLDEN RULES for growing a business

Constantly assess and reassess your business

There are four quadrants to a business: customers, suppliers, staff, and stakeholders. You make money when all four are in balance. If one is out of kilter, you don't have a square, you have a rhombus. Make sure you are constantly checking to ensure that these four groups are all operating as they should be, and then focus on the ones that aren't, to get them all back to equilibrium.

Be prepared

Always carry some form of payment with you because you never know when you might need it. I carry a company cheque book with me at all times – and my passport – in case I ever need it. I also always, always, always have business cards on me – whether it's

---

during the week, weekends or on holiday. You never know who you might meet and where you might meet them.

Don't let the numbers rule

Accountants are trained to believe that numbers are everything. And certainly, when you are running a business, it is invaluable to have a finance director who can bring them to life. The problem with the idea that the numbers mean everything though, is that it leaves aside emotion, perceptions and sometimes even the reality of a given situation.

Accountants will say that you need to increase sales and reduce costs, but, in business, you also need to take risks and factor in intangible matters, such as people's feelings. Even though cutting costs might seem effective in generating profit on a spreadsheet, in reality it can be counterproductive and occasionally investment might be wiser.

Chris Hanson, my finance director and subsequently chief operating officer at Cardpoint, summed it up best. He said that entrepreneurs look for ways to change things and create situations – they go into battle, lead from the front, plan risky strategies and inspire people to do things they'd never dreamt of doing. Then the accountants follow behind and bayonet the wounded. Make sure to always be the entrepreneur.

Ditch the status quo

Not changing anything is **not** an option. If you want to be successful, trying to maintain a successful situation is the equivalent of treading water in a fast-flowing river – standing still actually represents going backwards. Once you have your business running, momentum gives it a strength and purpose, which is addictive.

At one point, we decided to compare our stockbrokers against others in the market. We whittled it down to staying with our existing brokers or changing to another we had found. Both came to our board meeting at a Manchester Airport hotel and, at the end, I said to the board, "Well, there's nothing in it. Both are excellent and our existing broker will do just as good a job as a new one. There is no reason to change." Then I finished by saying, "So we will change, as the status quo is no good to anyone."

Alastair Richardson, my longstanding employee, used to complain that just when we'd settled things down, I'd challenge them and push for change. There is a reason I did that. Not only does it help the business, but I think it creates a more dynamic, interesting workplace.

Strike while the iron is hot

Sometimes you see something that just won't sell. It could be a property, a business or just about anything. However, as soon as you decide to buy it, it becomes hugely popular and you either end up bidding against somebody for it or, days after you've bought it, someone wants to buy it from you.

It seems that your decision to buy it gives others the comfort they needed to try and buy it themselves. If you've bought something that nobody else seems to want and then somebody offers you a handsome profit to sell it, it might be worth doing just that. Making a quick profit is gratifying and obviously financially rewarding. But don't wait too long.

Adopt a default upbeat attitude

My brother Nigel and I used to say the words 'onwards and upwards' to each other in tough times as well as good times. Somehow it spurred us on to greater things and ensured that we never took our foot off the accelerator. When we had to close down our first business, Prestige, we walked home together that evening to the terraced house we had converted into three flats. Nigel dropped a pint of milk at the top of the stairs and said, "It never rains, it pours." But that saying was too negative for us, so we vowed never to use it again.

Travel light

Travelling light has many meanings. I've only ever travelled with hand luggage to the US after my first trip there, when I landed in New York and my suitcase arrived in Washington. Less literally, travelling light applies to the amount of clutter on your desk, the files you archive, the number of core staff you employ, the number of vehicles you own and even the number of bank accounts you operate. All of these in any volume create work in themselves and, most of the time, the work they create is absolutely unnecessary and just wastes time.

On another level, when you're about to negotiate with someone, clearing your mind of assumptions, pre-conceived ideas and irrelevancies allows clear and directed thoughts to flow more freely. I hate irrelevancies or emotions being brought into discussion because they, again, waste time.

Write a business plan for your main competitor

Imagine you are running your main competitor's business instead of yours and write a business plan from their point of view, considering the opportunities and challenges that lie ahead. Looking at your market through their eyes will really help you see it more clearly. You will be surprised at how useful this exercise can be in shaping your own business plan. Generally in business, putting yourself into other people's shoes is a great idea and ensures that you act logically when trying to negotiate. It's also always worth thinking about how you would see yourself from the other person's perspective.

Dealing with Press and Government

When we announced the deal with Securicor, we were taken by surprise at how much interest it generated in the press. We had a big night out celebrating the deal and the following morning, when the press release was sent out, I turned on my phone to find 30 voice messages and 75 missed calls. Then I checked the share price to discover that it had shot up from 53p to 72p.

Clearly, everyone thought it was the best deal since sliced bread. I ended up spending the day talking to journalists and was so busy that I had to ask our chairman, Peter Smyth, to do a live slot on television. Unfortunately, Peter was so hungover from celebrations the night before that he could barely speak, left in the middle of the interview, walked in front of the camera on his way out and totally messed the whole thing up – much to our amusement.

We gradually integrated the Securicor machines into our own estate with the help of Roy Dodd, who joined us from there. Then, after we were up and running, we faced an unexpected challenge: Woolwich had been acquired by Barclays and Mick McHale contacted us to say they could no longer sponsor us. Woolwich wanted to get out of the sponsorship it operated with us and other cash machine operators, such as Moneybox, because cash machines that charged for withdrawals had begun to attract negative publicity.

It was not just the idea of charging users a fee to withdraw money that people didn't like, there was also speculation that it may lead to banks charging their own customers for withdrawals too. And there was a further complicating factor. At the time, some banks charged their customers a disloyalty fee for making withdrawals from other banks' cash machines, so there was also the unfounded fear that people might be charged twice for withdrawing money from another bank or, indeed, one of our machines.

We had liked working with Woolwich, not least because they did a lot of the work behind the scenes to run our cash machines, and their withdrawal meant that we would have to employ more people and join LINK in our own right, at considerable expense. We were rather cross about their decision to end the sponsorship. We'd also become good friends with Mick and his team.

There was a silver lining though. During the negotiations with Woolwich, they had attributed a lot of value to the fact that we could – and were actually required to – use the Woolwich logo. Whilst they were all involved with Woolwich as employees, advisors and so on, and thought that the Woolwich name carried lots of weight, I kept trying to explain that somebody living 500 miles away in the north of Scotland would have never even heard of the Woolwich, let alone attribute a brand value to the name.

Their belief in the intrinsic value of the brand did ultimately prove profitable to me, however. In order that we reach agreement with Woolwich to release them from their obligations in sponsoring us, we had to agree a deed of variation. We simply echoed their view about the value of the brand back to them, saying that our business would be decimated if it was not able to display the Woolwich logo and all that it stood for on the side of our cash machines.

Frank Shephard, the lawyer who had helped with the original negotiations, and I were despatched that evening to draft the deed and return the next day with it. As we were staying at the same hotel in London, Frank and I agreed to have our sensible heads on, only have a quick meal and a drink at the hotel and then draft the deed. However, as often happened with Frank, one drink led to another and I persuaded Frank to go out. We ended up out on the town and making it back to the hotel at 5am with no deed drafted. Ever the professional, Frank fired up his laptop and drafted the deed whilst sitting on my bed, even though we were both a bit the worse for wear. By 6.30am it was done and at 9am we were back at Woolwich's office, feeling slightly tired but with an expertly drafted deed in hand thanks to Frank.

Woolwich accepted our draft deed of variation and paid us handsomely for our loss of brand value. To show there were no hard feelings, we arranged a massive party for what seemed like most of Woolwich's staff. Mick McHale has told me since that we were the only people he knew who actually threw a party to celebrate the end of a relationship. But it felt like the right thing to do.

A year or two later, I managed to tempt Mick away from Woolwich to join the Board at Cardpoint. Mick was a worthy addition to Cardpoint, adding a great deal of value with his banking knowledge, as well as adding to our credibility in financial circles. He stayed on the Board to the very end.

The end of sponsorship by Woolwich led to us officially joining LINK, which turned out to be a very good thing anyway. I even became friendly with the CEO, John Hardy, and would regularly remind him about the times he refused to take my calls. In total, we invested just under £2m of our own funds into Cardpoint to ensure it stood on its own two feet following the withdrawal of Woolwich.

Meanwhile, there were more deals to be done. Having spent years trying to persuade the high street banks to sell all or part of their off-site cash machine estates to us, I eventually received a call out of the blue while on holiday near Loch Ness.

It was from a man at Halifax Bank of Scotland (HBOS). It transpired that our arch rivals at Moneybox had done a much better job than us of persuading HBOS to dispose of their cash machine estate, but, for corporate governance reasons and to show fair play, HBOS wanted to check that Moneybox's intentions were reasonable and that any offer would be at an appropriate level.

I knew that the implications and benefit to Moneybox of making such an acquisition were huge. Moneybox was set to demerge from Ambient plc and list in its own right on AIM and the HBOS deal would have been a real coup for them.

We were obviously keen to acquire the HBOS cash machines for ourselves and it turned out that we had an ace up our sleeves. One of my non-executive directors had introduced me to the blue-blooded bank, N M Rothschild & Sons Limited, and we had held many meetings with Andy Thomas there in which I outlined my vision for the business. As soon as we started negotiating with HBOS we mentioned the Rothschild connection – we were later told that this really helped to persuade HBOS to take us seriously.

I discovered early on in the process that we were only bidding against Moneybox and that nobody else was left in the running. This was partly because I was invited to a meeting on the outskirts of Edinburgh and discovered in the visitors' book that Moneybox's CEO had signed in 90 minutes earlier. When I sign a visitors' book, I make sure that it's illegible and use initials for the company. I reckon that if you have to evacuate the building you can always apologise afterwards.

The deal itself turned into a nightmare. After dealing with Dermot Desmond and being pleasantly surprised, HBOS threw so many curve balls into the deal that it was hard to tell left from right. Not least, after months of negotiation it turned out that their contracts with the retailers for the provision of cash machines were all signed up in the wrong legal entity. This meant that at the eleventh hour the whole deal had to be restructured and a huge deferred element had to be introduced – something which gave both Rothschild and our brokers, the renamed Evolution Beeson Gregory, cause for concern.

At one point somebody joked that HBOS must need the money… and a few years later, during the financial crisis, it certainly looked like they had needed as much money as possible.

It turned out well in the end, though, and we paid HBOS approximately £52m for the cash machines, raising £45m by placing new shares at £1.25 and increasing our debt facility with HBOS to pay for the acquisition.

Integrating the cash machines into our existing estate was hard work, but over time we managed to persuade the retailers of 300 machines, out of 816, to allow us to convert them to charging machines, so the deal paid off. We continued to operate the rest as non-charging machines, partly because the cash going through them boosted our overall volumes, so helped us to reduce our own costs of getting cash, and partly as a goodwill gesture. If a machine was the last one in a town, I felt it would have been a bit mean to start charging for withdrawals. However, I had no idea then that such a great deal would soon cause me a large furore.

There are two things to avoid in business. The first one is injunctions: injunctions against you are very, very bad. Fortunately, I've never been served with one, but I've obtained a few.

The second one is a Treasury Select Committee. To be summoned to a Treasury Select Committee is never a great day out.

My calling came at the end of 2004. Politicians had always been incensed by the idea of charging cash machines because they felt it was wrong to charge people to withdraw their own money. The fact that HBOS had sold 816 cash machines, that had provided free withdrawals, to a company that charged for withdrawals, had really set the cat among the pigeons. It was further complicated by the fact that HBOS had lent us £30m to make the acquisition. I could see the misunderstanding of how deals worked etched on the MPs' faces and the then CEO of HBOS, James Crosby, was given a real grilling over it.

The main contention against us was that customers were being duped into paying to use our machines – despite the signage on and around the machines and the fact that customers had to accept the charge by answering yes to the question: 'do you accept the withdrawal fee charge of £1.50?'

From our own research, we knew that users of our machines were fully aware of the fee they had to pay to withdraw money, they had just decided that the small charge was more than offset by the time and/or money they saved in finding an alternative machine. Nevertheless, politicians and the *Daily Mail* were united in their belief that customers were being wronged and that it was an outrage. Every six weeks or so, the *Daily Mail* would run another story saying how many charging cash machines there were and how they were a disgrace.

The MP John McFall led the charge and, while he claimed to have consumers' interests at heart, in my opinion the whole process was based on a technical misunderstanding and, in the end, cost money without benefiting anybody. It was a fairly stressful experience and involved endless meetings at the House of Commons with various organisations. One meeting had a government minister and representatives from just about every consumer body in the UK, yet the only people present from the actual industry were myself and a guy from the Royal Bank of Scotland, which owned a subsidiary with charging cash machines.

On the day of the final hearing, I took a call from Andrew Martin, who ran our German cash machine business. He wisely said, "Just enjoy it! You'll probably never do it again and it'll be a great experience."

I heeded his advice and immediately relaxed. I was sandwiched between three CEOs of my main rivals: Ron Delnevo of Bank Machine; Peter McNamara, the Chairman of Moneybox; and Ashley Dean of TRM.

At one point, McFall held up a piece of paper displaying the message which forewarned cash machine users that they are about to incur charges. He asked the four of us, in turn, to read the writing on it. It was impossible to read from so far away but, when it was my turn, I recited the exact wording back to him. He looked astonished and rather cross – especially when I told him that I knew what it said because I'd written it. Everyone in the gallery laughed and I began to enjoy myself.

The whole investigation turned out to be a lot of hot air, as the findings were benign and didn't affect our customers or usage in any way. I was briefly featured on the *News at Ten* though.

The experience taught me that although people sometimes have good intentions, this can be irrelevant if the people they think they are serving don't feel aggrieved. Our own research showed that users saw the fee they were charged as value for money, considering the time it would take them to find an alternative machine. It was also clear that our users agreed to pay for something that they could obtain for free, so the claim that our customers were being duped into paying simply didn't stack up.

There was another benefit to the *Daily Mail's* campaign against us. Every time they ran a piece saying that cash machine charges were a disgrace, our usage would actually go up, because they were basically advertising our machines and telling people where to find them. I would often bump into customers who would tell me that they never knew there was a charging cash machine in their local Spar shop until they read about it in the *Daily Mail*, and how handy it was to have one there. For us, there was no such thing as bad publicity and, as far as I was concerned, the more the *Daily Mail* wrote about us, the better.

My GOLDEN RULES for creating a winning attitude

Walk the walk and talk the talk

Research has shown that if you saw the pilot of the plane you were flying on emerge from the cockpit in jeans and a T-shirt, your confidence in them would fall. But, if the same person was smartly dressed in uniform and had a good posture, you would feel more confident that they were able to command the aircraft.

Presenting a certain impression of yourself works in two ways. Understanding them will have a big impact on your ability to succeed.

Firstly, it will fill you with self-confidence. If you wish to portray yourself as a successful marketeer of your new product, for example, then you should look, act and talk like somebody who has been successfully marketing for years. In this way, makeover programmes are fascinating to watch, simply because by changing people's outward appearance, they walk taller, demonstrate better posture, look more relaxed and are generally more successful. You cannot underestimate the effect that dressing appropriately will have on your own performance.

Also, I don't subscribe to the notion of 'I'm an individual and true to myself, so I never wear a suit'. Even if not wearing a suit *did* make you seem more individual, is independence of thought something that those around you are actually seeking? If you turn up to see your bank manager dressed in jeans while asking for funds to start your own high-powered business consultancy, are they going to take you seriously?

Secondly, it will inspire confidence in the people you are interacting with. For instance, when you go to see a potential customer, bank manager, key supplier or investor, they will have already decided what they expect from you. Meeting these expectations will start the relationship off on the right foot.

When you walk into a room and shake hands, the other party will assess you and immediately think, 'Serious business person, successful, obviously switched on.' Your meeting will already be off to a flying start and their thought process might also add '…and I'd like to be like them.' This is significant because if someone wants to be like you they will adjust to your wavelength and subconsciously suppress any negative thoughts they may harbour about what you're about to say.

Dressing well also serves a further purpose. During my time at Cardpoint, we had a falling out with a company that we allowed to transact withdrawals through our cash machines. It ended up in mediation, which mostly consists of shuttling in and out of meetings trying to agree on matters, on a very hot day in an office with no air conditioning. Every time we went into a meeting, we had suits on with our ties done up – even though as soon as we left we quickly disrobed. By the end of the day, our opponents were frazzled and looked it. We achieved a great outcome, thanks to Steve Morris, our expert litigation lawyer, and the excellent David Casement QC, who was our barrister, but I always in part believed that because we looked professional and cool that this gradually wore our opponents down.

In my experience, you will succeed far more if you meet and beat people's expectations than if you portray yourself as eccentric or esoteric. If you want to dress like a hoodie or a rapper, do it at home.

Put the effort in

Success takes hard work, which can involve immense personal sacrifice. At Postal Facilities, it took two and a half years of blood, sweat and tears before we managed to install our first postbox. It took a further two years to sell the business – I lost count of how many meetings I had in London with accountants, lawyers and potential purchasers. I was working at the Insurance & Legal advertising business to earn an income, at Postal Facilities to generate a capital gain and then constantly dealing with the Royal Mail, petrol companies and advertisers.

I was away so much that one night when I finally managed to ring home just after midnight, I felt compelled to reassure my wife of my feelings. When she sleepily answered, I said, "I just wish I was with you now, holding you close, feeling your soft skin against mine, about to make love to you, rather than being in this hotel on my own." She replied, "Who is this?" At least she hadn't lost her sense of humour in my absence.

But success also requires you to work smart as well as hard. When the Postal Facilities sale was completed, I bumped into one of my cousins who said, "Bit of luck, that, selling that business." "Really?" I replied disbelievingly. He smiled, "Yes, I mean, come on, you've only put six boxes up."

I just stared at him and resisted the urge to laugh. Then I explained, patiently, that although there is an element of luck in every achievement, there is always a far greater proportion of hard work in it.

If you're in the room, be in the room

If you're playing in the garden with your children half-heartedly because you're thinking about work, or staring at pictures of your family on your desk while you are at work, you need to adjust. If you've invested the time to watch your children's sports day, you may as well immerse yourself in it; think of nothing else, just enjoy it and let your kids see you concentrating on them, shouting for them and clapping. As a child, would you have wanted your parent to be talking into a phone at the side of the field, not taking any notice and just being there in body, not spirit?

Similarly, if you're in a meeting, concentrate on that, not on the things you need to deal with next. Be in the room – you'll work better, live better and be liked more.

Stop talking about your problems

I was once told that if you have a problem, 50% of the people you tell couldn't care less, 49% of them are glad that you have the problem rather than them, and 1% are bothered about the problem. Guess what? The 1% are your family and true friends. The moral of this is that 99% of the time you're wasting your breath telling somebody about a problem. You'd be better off investing that time into solving it.

Surround yourself with like-minded people

You need to make sure that the people around you have your best interests at heart. As you become more successful, you will attract advisors and people who, whilst they would never admit it, just want to be aligned with your success. Some people have no ulterior motive, but others may want to befriend you for their own advantage. Putting it bluntly, most people will never make a million and, as compensation, want to become friends with someone who has. It makes a great topic of conversation to be able to say, "Oh yes, I've known so-and-so for years, worth a fortune. One of my best friends in fact…"

Indeed, there are two specific categories you'll experience. One is the set of so-called friends, who hold onto the idea that if they ever run into trouble financially then they will at least have a rich friend who can bail them out. The second set seem to think that by associating with a successful, millionaire entrepreneur, that they will learn the magic formula from you. It's as though they think there is some sort of secret which you'll blurt out in front of them, and then they can run home, do something and the money will roll in.

Perhaps not surprisingly, I have found that most successful people have very few genuine friends. The truth is that you tend to end up being friends with those who knew you before you enjoyed success, because these are the only people who you know in your heart of hearts like *you* rather than what you've achieved, have or can share with them.

The most successful people I've met never stop moving forward and carry a confidence that every year business will surpass the last. This gives them a momentum which seems to carry them into the next deal, regardless of other events. They believe in themselves and their abilities, and always have an open mind that is receptive to ideas and opportunities.

The converse is also true. If you hear anyone saying: "I'll never do as well as that again", "I'll never find another idea as good", "Those were the days" or "It was different then", they've applied the brakes to themselves. Make sure you are spending your time with the kind of people who will boost, rather than drain, your energy.

Resist peer pressure

As your business grows, you may find yourself under pressure to replicate the behaviour of other people in your industry. For example, if a particular industry has an annual dinner for all the key people and everyone goes without their partners and gets drunk, there will be a huge amount of pressure for you to do the same. Yet if you attend with your partner and you both stay sober, you'll risk alienation even though you may capture the moral high ground.

The decision of whether to go and participate, go and take the moral high ground or avoid the occasion altogether is a tricky one. You need to decide whether to allow other people's behaviour to influence your own. Sometimes participation is more appropriate than avoidance – but not where your integrity is compromised. I am always happy to have a few drinks at social events, for instance, but I draw the line at taking an illegal substance. I can proudly say that I've never had any experience with drugs because my business and family provide enough highs.

When people discuss their success, it typically gets narrowed down to the business domain: customer service, selling things, staff, accounts, banks and all that good stuff. No one ever mentions the *soft* decisions you'll have to make along the way, that you may have previously decided on in a purely personal capacity.

The fact is that success comes with responsibility. You are the leader of a business and you need to demonstrate your personal integrity, whether that is to your customers, suppliers or employees. If you are honest and true to yourself then you can expect the same of others – the opposite is also true.

Smile

I've never had much time for moody or sulky people. I always smile because it puts people at ease and it just makes for a nicer atmosphere. If you are under loads of pressure and you look grumpy, that rubs off on people, so make the effort to smile even if you don't feel like smiling.

Even if I had had a shocking day, I would go out into our big open office at Cardpoint and be Mr Happy Smiley, because I wanted everyone to feel that everything was alright. I didn't want them to go, "Oh crikey, the boss looks like the world has ended, I think I might get another job." I genuinely think this has helped people to stay with us, even in the tough times. We are naturally attracted to people who smile so, unless you intend to be a catwalk model, leave the sad face at home and spend time smiling instead.

Identify things that motivate and inspire you

I used to work in an office in Blackpool that overlooked a B&Q

store, but then I realised that I could just as easily work from home in some converted stables and look out at a fantastic view every day instead. I sold the offices and now I have the sun beaming in through the windows and I can see pheasants in the garden. Try to find an environment to work in that motivates you and inspires you to do deals and grow a business.

Moneybox

In the summer of 2005, we made our boldest move of all – we acquired our arch rival Moneybox, a much bigger business than ours, for £87.3m. We funded the deal by selling 43.3m Cardpoint shares, to raise £55m, and increasing our loan from the Bank of Scotland for £75m. I couldn't have done it without the help of my new finance director, Robin Gregson, and Chris Hanson, who had moved into the role of chief operating officer.

The deal gave us a total of 6,000 machines, making us the biggest operator of fee-charging cash machines in the UK. In transaction terms, we were now one of the biggest operators in the world. Acquiring Moneybox also took us further into Germany and Holland, where their machines had been installed and we too had started operations. As I said in a press release at the time: "Moneybox has built a strong market position in the UK, Germany and the Netherlands, and we intend to solidify the enlarged group's positioning further by combining the key strengths of both businesses."

Buying Moneybox was the best strategic deal I ever made because it meant that we basically dominated the market and had no one to be played off against. When customers said they thought they could get a better deal than the one we were offering, they would ring the Moneybox number and just get through to me again on my other phone number.

We did have to get clearance from the Monopolies and Mergers Commission, now called the Competition Commission, to go ahead with the deal. They approved it after concluding that Cardpoint acquiring Moneybox made no difference to the end user of our machines, because if they were prepared to pay to use them, they were going to pay regardless of who owned them. The only people who could possibly be disenfranchised by the move were shop owners, but as we provided our machines to them for free, we couldn't do any more than that.

It was, nevertheless, an enormous acquisition for us which presented the considerable challenge of having to integrate both businesses into one, single identity. Many of the roles within the business were suddenly duplicated and it was clear that we were going to have to make about 100 redundancies to reduce the total workforce down to around 300. But I didn't want to make any hasty decisions, so I told everyone that their jobs would be safe for at least six months until after Christmas. I also reassured them that we would help them find new jobs and that is exactly what we did.

I spoke to three of our suppliers and found jobs with them for everyone we needed to let go. No one burst into tears or called me names; instead I received thank you cards from people saying I had handled it really well and that they were really happy in their new jobs. Afterwards, everyone told me that it was the nicest redundancy they had ever been through.

Meanwhile, I needed to decide what to do about Moneybox's team of 50 maintenance engineers, whose job it was to go around servicing cash machines. We had outsourced our machine maintenance to Securicor when we acquired their machines. So, on the face of it, it seemed logical to dismiss the inherited maintenance team and outsource upkeep of the Moneybox machines to Securicor as well. I had even promised our institutional shareholders that we would save £500,000 a year by doing this, as the team cost £2.5m to run and Securicor would only charge us £2m to take over the work.

However, I had a niggling feeling that I shouldn't rush into doing this and, since I had promised staff their jobs for the next six months anyway, I arranged to spend a day out with one of them as he drove around in his van repairing machines.

The poor man was a nervous wreck at the idea of spending an entire day alone with the chief executive so, when I climbed into his van in my jeans and T-shirt, I told him that the way we were going to do this was that I would simply be Mark for the day and he would just be Tony. I would be his assistant if he needed me to hold the screwdriver or whatever.

Tony was a lovely guy and we ended up having a real laugh together. He had been working the same patch for several years and knew all the machines he was repairing really well.

The day out with Tony got me thinking, and I decided to introduce some changes to the way the maintenance team worked. I told them that I wanted them to start repairing the machines for the long term rather than going back every month to fix the same problem with a short-term solution. If a machine kept breaking down, I wanted them to either replace the broken part or replace the entire machine. Above all, I wanted them to feel responsible for the machines they looked after, be less reactive and more proactive, so that more of our machines would be working perfectly at any one time and our customers would have a much better experience.

I also gave them uniforms. Whenever I walked into a corner shop in a suit the owner would instantly notice me and stop serving other customers to ask how they could help. But when I was out with Tony, he wasted a lot of time standing in queues waiting to be noticed before he could start repairing a machine, because he didn't stand out in any way. I had jackets made for everyone. They didn't say Cardpoint on them, because I didn't want anyone hitting them over the head thinking that they were carrying large amounts of cash, but they looked a lot smarter and were more noticeable. This enabled the team to visit more machines, therefore completing more repairs, each day. Similarly, I improved the technology in the vans.

Within weeks I realised that, despite my earlier plans to outsource the work to Securicor, it actually made more sense to keep the team on.

I did just that, and it worked so well that I eventually unwound our agreement with Securicor and brought all the maintenance in-house. When I spoke to institutional investors about this decision, I explained that we were actually saving more money than we would have done by outsourcing the maintenance. On top of that, we were increasing the number of machines that were in operation at any given time, which improved the service we were able to offer our customers. By the end, our machines had an availability rate of 99.5%, which was the highest in the industry.

This experience taught me that even if a decision seems obvious it is always worth looking at from a different angle, because you might be surprised by what you discover.

As I was doing so much travelling for work, it made sense to employ a full-time driver to take me from my home in Lytham to our London office and around to meetings during the day. They could also shuttle me to and from the airport when I had to go overseas. This meant I could work in the car as well as hold private conversations, which I couldn't do on the train.

Employing a driver was not without its hazards, though. My first driver used to stay down in London during the week in the same hotel as me because I found it useful having a driver in London. But one evening, he decided to drive the 240 miles back to Lytham to briefly see his wife. The following morning, he didn't leave enough time to return to London to collect me from the hotel and ended up driving 100 miles an hour in fog to try to make up the time – he was stopped by the police for dangerous driving. That was the end of his time working for me. As I explained to him, it wasn't about my car or being late, I was more bothered about him hurting himself if he had a crash.

Another chauffeur was a fantastic driver, but he had a bladder the size of a walnut and we were always having to stop for the toilet. He couldn't even drive past Charnock Richard services, about 40 minutes out of Lytham, without needing to stop for a break. I nicknamed him Terry the Toilet. He also forgot that I was in the car once. I had been quiet for a couple of hours and when he came off the motorway he decided to really go for it on some country lanes. It's pretty difficult to work with a laptop on your knee while you are being thrown around in the backseat and going round corners at 75 miles an hour.

My GOLDEN RULES for managing your employees

Always follow procedure

It's vital to follow the correct procedure when dealing with employees. I once suffered a situation which would not have been out of place in the hit TV comedy, *The Office*. We had an utterly useless employee, inherited through an acquisition, who managed to survive in his role despite my strong feelings. This was mainly because I have always believed in consensus, and allowed my managers and directors to make decisions and collectively overrule me.

However, matters started to come to a head and he showed his true colours. I kept urging one of my directors to give him an 'off the record' talking to, then a verbal warning, then a written warning, and so on. But the employee didn't improve and had to go. The director agreed with me and said he'd sack him. About two weeks later, though, I spotted the employee in the office. I called the director in and asked why he'd given the employee so long to clear his desk and leave.

After a few minutes of stuttering and stammering, the director finally admitted that although he had given all of the requisite warnings, he hadn't actually dismissed the employee. We agreed to call the employee in and sort the matter out there and then. The director continued to delay and refused to fetch the employee, suggesting that he'd deal with him later. "Enough," I said, and went and found the employee myself, dragging him into my office.

"OK. You've been given a verbal, written and final written warning, yet things clearly haven't improved," I said. "No, I haven't been given any of those warnings," he replied. I turned to the director, who was looking out of the window, and said, "You told me that we'd been through all the procedures." But, as it turned out, this wasn't the case. The employee left the business, having been paid his due notice period.

So what happened to the director?

Well, I obviously sacked him too. He left the office immediately, but resolving the situation was a lot more complicated. I offered him exactly the amount he was due, but he wrote to ask for considerably more. He later said that as I would not accept his request, I would be hearing from his solicitors.

The next couple of months were spent receiving vitriolic letters from his solicitors demanding instant replies. However, since I had lots of other things to deal with, I felt that he was the least of my worries and every time the deadline to reply approached, I asked for more time.

Eventually we reached a compromise, but the whole ordeal wasted a lot of time and money. It did teach me a valuable lesson though. If the director had been employed in the business during this time, we would have met at 9am and worked through the paperwork until an agreement was reached. I would have signed everything and given him a cheque and he'd have ridden off into the sunset.

As it was, his absence lowered his significance to me, making it easier for me to prioritise everything else above him. In the end, it was only sorted because we couldn't be bothered with a court case and needed to draw a line under the situation.

Stand your ground

My faith in employees and good nature has been tested many times over the years, but never more so than when I had to dismiss an errant secretary. I always gave staff time off between Christmas and New Year but asked them to come in, dressed casually, to tidy up, deal with outstanding items and generally take time to catch up. However, this particular secretary didn't turn up and instead rang in to say she was too ill to come in.

The following day, the phone rang at work. It was her. She was surprised I had answered, but we were on skeleton staff. She asked for the finance director, saying crossly that her wages hadn't gone into her bank account. I explained that we normally pay salaries on the 23rd of each month, but because that was a Saturday and

Christmas Day and Boxing Day fell on the Monday and Tuesday, her wages wouldn't leave our bank until Wednesday 27th December.

I could hear that she was at the till in a shop so I added, "But, anyway, you rang yesterday to say you were too ill to work, so you can't be out and about spending money, can you? So, as you've lied, we'll call it a day and you can collect your things tomorrow." With that, she hung up.

The following day, my office door burst open. It was the secretary. "Mills, only you would sack somebody between Christmas and New Year. You're a ruthless, unkind bastard!" she shouted. I replied, "It's too late for flattery, you won't sweet talk me into giving you your job back just by paying me compliments." She stormed out. It was a great retort but nobody else heard it – always the way.

Act decisively

Luckily, I've only had one really nasty situation. At Cardpoint we had a large, open-plan office, a deliberate choice made to encourage communication. I loved sitting and chatting to everybody together, telling them my ideas and listening to theirs, sharing (bad) jokes, making presentations and doing exercises, running competitions and generally messing about.

One Friday, I returned to the office after having been out all week. As usual, I walked around but sensed a very dark mood. Nobody was forthcoming about what was wrong. I tried asking people in private, but everyone clammed up. I rang my co-directors. Chris Hanson told me that two of the lads who worked for me had hacked into the email system and could read everyone's emails. Due to lack of evidence, they hadn't been confronted.

Against my lawyers' advice I summoned them to the boardroom.

They were visibly shaking, as this was a rare occurrence. I'd read that people's stress levels shoot up if they're called in to see the boss, even though he may have good news, so I would normally go to fetch people myself and say, "Can I see you for five minutes about something great/positive that you'll enjoy hearing about." Everybody would then relax and walk to my office smiling, which was much more productive. If I needed to talk about something that wasn't good, I would just say, "Can I have a private chat?"

In the boardroom, the two email hackers denied everything and promised that they would never do anything of the sort. I sent them back to their desks and within 20 minutes found evidence that proved they were lying. It also emerged that a girl in the office had found out what they had done and they had threatened to say it was her. It had now turned into a bullying situation, which I abhor. I demanded that they return to the boardroom and asked if they wanted a witness. They said no, so I said, well I do, and called in my PA Diana, who is still with me after 16 years. I asked Diana to transcribe exactly what was said.

"You're both dismissed immediately for gross misconduct, give me your door passes and get out of my building!" I shouted. "Did you note that down?" I asked Diana.

"Yes," she replied, sheepishly. "Thank you," I said and walked the lads to the door. I never heard from them again.

I went to the main office, gathered everyone together and told them what I'd done. Two girls burst into tears because they'd suffered all week and were so relieved to hear that I'd acted. They were disappointed that nobody had acted sooner but were glad that as soon as I was aware of the goings-on, I had acted decisively. An important lesson to learn is that, when it comes to employment matters, you should always act immediately and decisively.

Don't play the alienation game

If you've built a team and someone isn't performing, your mentioning it to their colleagues will start up whispers. People rarely defend someone that the boss feels negatively towards because it might make them look bad. They instead start to report this person's every minor failing or misdemeanour, things that would normally be overlooked for those within the team or 'inner sanctum'.

A bit like in the school playground, everybody slowly but surely turns against the person you've identified, alienating them in the process.

If this happens, it means **you have failed as a boss**. This game should never be played and, if you find it happening at your workplace, you should do everything you can to stop it immediately.

It has taken a long time to eradicate this behaviour within my organisations. Not an easy task, considering that people deny that such behaviour exists, deny that they 'joined in', and can justify their actions because the people in question were wrong anyway. However, the ends don't justify the means.

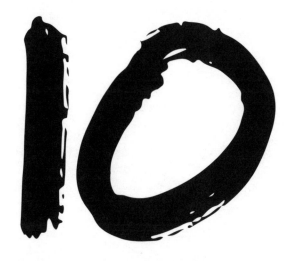

Goodbye Cardpoint

Everything was going brilliantly. We'd acquired Moneybox and begun to successfully integrate the two businesses. As a result, we had a dominant share of the market.

And then, suddenly, it wasn't going so brilliantly. Before we bought Moneybox, we were on track to make pre-tax profits of £14m that year. Moneybox was expected to make profits of £10m. So the City analysts do what they always do and added £10m to £14m and came up with a profit forecast of £30m for the combined group, on the spurious grounds that when we put the two businesses together we were going to be able to take out £6m of costs. But our bank, which knew our business better than anyone, was only expecting us to make a combined profit of £20m because Moneybox was not in good shape and had already issued a profits warning.

So, guided by our bank, we went round telling our shareholders that they should work on the assumption that we were going to make profits of around £20m. As we were a publicly listed company, we weren't allowed to give actual forecasts without making a formal statement to the market, so we asked them to listen to what the brokers were saying, look at the bank's assumptions and draw their own conclusions.

The problem was that because the brokers had said we were going to make profits of £30m, we then had to issue a formal profits warning, explaining that our profits would be closer to £20m. That meant we received a real panning from our shareholders and the share price dropped back from around £1.30 to 70p. To salvage the situation, I agreed to spend the following year grinding out profit from Moneybox rather than pursuing acquisitions.

I did exactly that and when we announced that we had made profits of £20m (on a turnover of £98m), we were approached by an Icelandic private-equity firm who were interested in buying the business.

I was at Oktoberfest, the huge beer festival in Germany, with a group of friends when I received an envelope under the door of my hotel room. It was a fax from our advisors: the Icelandic firm had offered to buy the business for £1 a share. It was a fantastic offer, but I obviously couldn't tell anyone about it, so I just jumped around the hotel room on my own before going out to get drunk with the others.

When I returned from Germany, I visited our shareholders to find out what they thought about the offer. By then it had leaked out, as these things seem to, which was unhelpful because this put the pressure on to decide what we were going to do. I explained that I thought £1 a share was a good price for the business, given that the shares were then trading at 72p. Especially as all the shareholders had come in either at 43p, 53p or 72p.

But almost all of the big shareholders disagreed with me and flatly refused to accept the offer. They felt there was potential for the share price to go higher and wanted the business to continue as it was. It was incredibly frustrating as, despite many hours of discussion, there was nothing I could do to change their minds. There was no point in even formally putting the Icelandic offer to them because it had been made clear that they would reject it. After giving it a lot of thought, I reluctantly said that I would sell my shares and hand the business over to someone else to run.

After seven years at Cardpoint, it was time to bow out.

I started selling my shares, amounting to slightly less than 10% of the business, through my broker and, within six weeks of leaving, I had sold them all at an average share price of 92p. This gave me around

£5m. In total, I had made around £9m from Cardpoint, having turned my initial investment of £1m into £10m.

I was sort of glad to be out of the business, but felt frustrated that I had not been able to sell the business in its entirety or to give all my shareholders a one-time exit. I will always be immensely proud to have created and led Cardpoint, but, for me, the business had started to disobey the most golden rule – it had ceased to be fun. And when the fun has gone, it's time to go.

I always enjoyed being challenged and either winning the argument or being persuaded of a better course of action. Without a doubt, though, everyone performs better with like-minded individuals who respect you and aren't trying to prove something about their own inadequacies. In this way, I found that while certain non-executive directors quickly grasped issues and offered support and advice, others felt the need to intervene and try to dictate.

Part of the problem was to do with age. The directors I got on well with were a bit more switched on to the realities of a young 30-something running a dynamic business with 300 staff based in Blackpool. But those who were nearer my late grandfather's age could never keep up with the information flow and would reminisce about the days when board meetings ended at lunchtime and were followed by long drinks, an afternoon of mutual backslapping and dinner in the evening. To this day, I've only ever had a couple of seriously long lunches, all in celebration of a successful deal, and they were all more than deserved. In light of these experiences, when I advise other people, I always try to 'think young' and be in touch with current trends.

Before finally leaving the business, I met the man who was brought in to take over my CEO role and gave him three pieces of advice. First, don't close the Blackpool office: it's the heart and soul of the company, it's low-cost, everyone is committed and it runs like a well-oiled machine. Second, don't buy Travelex's cash machine estate because we have looked at it twice and it isn't worth buying. And third, don't merge with a company called Alphyra because it will benefit their business more than ours.

He didn't listen and within 12 months had done all three.

It took a while but sure enough the business started to decline, with the share price eventually collapsing to 1p. The business was then taken over by private equity and repackaged. Years later, the business was sold for £100m to Cardtronics, the biggest cashpoint machine business in the world. By chance, I was at an awards ceremony when the advisors who had handled the sale of Cardpoint to Cardtronics won an award for it. This was much to the amusement of the people on my table at the ceremony who found it odd to see me clapping enthusiastically about my old company. The shareholders never did see more than £1 for their shares, but I'm glad it's still going 19 years later.

My GOLDEN RULES for managing your money

Never forget the value of money

I love cars and replace the one I have with a newer model every few years. But, even now that I am well off, I never like buying brand-new cars because they are a total waste of money. I prefer to buy a car that would cost £100,000 brand new for just £70,000, with 2,000 miles on the clock. I recently bought a fully specced up S class Mercedes for £45,000 with 4,000 miles on the clock – a car that would have cost £70,000 new. In fact, it turned out to have been previously owned by Michael Flatley, the Riverdance guy, and that might be why the pedals are a bit worn out.

When I want to change my car, I simply sell it to the same local dealer who always gets me a better price than others. One day, he came to my house to buy my old car and, when he arrived at the door, he told me that he had picked up a fiver that was blowing down the drive. I said, "Nice one, I was telling Angela that I'd dropped a fiver somewhere and was looking for it."

He burst out laughing and said: "Millsy, why are you bothered about a fiver? Why do you care? You have lost £50,000 driving this car for three years and you are worried about a fiver?" I said: "Three people used to have to use my cash machines for me to make a fiver. I have been in a business where 0.2p was extremely important and would have affected the profits of the business. I am as bothered about losing a fiver as I was when I had absolutely nothing, because a fiver is still a fiver."

Never forget the value of money, no matter how much you manage to make of it. A fiver is still a fiver.

You only need one word to make a fortune

There is only one word you will ever need to become rich. And you will probably never guess it. That word is *save*. If you earn £100,000 per month and are spending every penny, you'll have a great standard of living but will never be truly rich. Yes, you'll be living a millionaire's lifestyle but, one day, if the income dries up, it's game over – unless you have been saving. And trust me, nothing lasts forever.

Never fool yourself that you are saving when you aren't. You need to be able to look at your bank account and see the balance rising month by month. The first step towards saving is to become debt-free. Even if you're not yet earning big money, do what I did and cut up all of your credit cards. If you have £10,000 of credit card borrowings, each year it will cost you £2,500 simply to stand still and avoid those debts getting worse. If you cut them up, thereby guaranteeing that you can't spend more, and work at paying them off, then you will find yourself better off in an almost turbo-charged fashion. First, once you reduce the debt to zero, you will save £2,500 each year. Second, when you go past zero and save £10,000, your bank will pay you for keeping it there.

Pay all debts off, starting this week, by living within your means. Once you're debt-free, put money away every week as soon as you can, without making excuses. You'll never, ever regret putting savings away and you'll enjoy the payment you receive for doing it.

I remember opening the post one morning, having saved and struggled to become debt-free (apart from my mortgage), and reading a bank statement that said we'd earned £1,000 in interest. In those days my wife and three children could go away for a fortnight with that amount. In effect, the bank were paying for our holiday. Is your bank paying for your holiday, or are you paying for the holiday of the boss of the credit card company? Which option would you prefer? Take action now and start saving.

Understand what's in it for you

The question, 'What's in it for me?' is not about being selfish – it's designed to save you time and/or money.

Whether you're selling a house, buying a car, ordering a new three-piece suit or even a pair of shoes, there can often be a delay or inconvenience to you. Delivery will take six weeks, the purchaser needs more time to complete his paperwork, the shop doesn't have the right colour or size in stock. You are then asked to be patient and wait for the goods or service to be delivered or provided at a time that suits the other party.

Take selling a house. If the purchasers have been slow to arrange their mortgage, your solicitor may ring three days before completion to say they need another week. Your solicitor will probably explain that it's unavoidable, that it happens frequently and, after all, it's only a week. But why should you give up something for nothing?

If you say yes, they have the benefit of more time and you've lost out on a week of living in your new home, or the cash from selling your property. So, if they want an extra week why not ask 'What's in it for me?' Your solicitor may bluster a bit but press on and insist he asks the other party for some sort of recognition for your generosity. In my experience, in the surprise of being asked, most people will panic and offer you more than you would expect. They may offer a one-off payment, to pay your expenses or even actually manage to meet the original timescale.

By asking the question, you have nothing to lose and something to gain. So, try it next time you're asked to give in on something. Then enjoy spending the extra money you're given or wearing the extra pair of socks the shoe shop throws in.

Tip big and early

If you tip after you've received great service, you're not paying for great service anymore.

On holiday, I always tip the guys who find us sunloungers by the pool on the first day and I make it a relatively substantial amount, say £20. This means that for the rest of the holiday they tend to spot me as I arrive at the pool and then find or direct me to sunloungers they've already reserved. I only need to tip them minimally again, if at all.

Perhaps I've been lucky, but this system has never let me down. In my opinion, it's more efficient than giving the guys a few quid and hoping each day that they come up trumps, especially as they don't know who you are and have no reason to remember you, and then rewarding them at the end of the holiday when they can do nothing more for you.

I've applied this concept to business in a similarly effective way. Customers have often dangled small pieces of business in front of me with the promise of bigger, better business to come. Invariably, they want me to price the first piece of work cheaply to show them how keen I am to secure the next, supposedly better, part. This is a dangerous route to take because, if you do this, not only will you set a bad precedent regarding your price – and therefore profitability – but you may never receive the big prize anyway. In fact, given the marginal, unprofitable nature of the piece of business, the company will hardly be likely to prioritise or throw extra resources at it.

When I am looking to award business to a supplier, I go about it in a very different, more effective, way. I give them the first piece of business at a great profit margin. This lets them show you everything they're capable of at full strength. It endears the supplier to you, rather than creating resentment on their side because they are having to do a piece of business for no profit. It also gives you a positive lead-in for the future.

Importantly, when you're negotiating the price or fees for the bigger piece of business, you have more leverage to reduce the price you're paying, as they know you are a good customer and have already made a profit from you. You can also tell them that as they now know how you work, they should be able to figure out where they can reduce costs – without cutting corners – and still make a profit.

Always negotiate the price

If you are buying something, you should never accept the first price you are quoted. When Nigel and I were selling our postbox business, Postal Facilities, we'd had lots of interest that had come to nothing. When we finally received a fantastic offer, I told Nigel that we shouldn't accept it.

He argued that whilst our belief that we should never accept the first offer had stood us in good stead so far, that this was different. But I won the argument, so we rejected the offer. The following week, Nigel scowled at me every day, reminding me that the phone wasn't ringing. I never told him, but I was barely sleeping either. However, I was confident that the other side would come back with a better offer because they had already invested time, effort and money into negotiating the deal and, importantly, had agreed the deal in principle at a board meeting.

The week after we'd rejected the knock-out offer, I was summoned to see the buyer's team. They had been working on the deal day and night and now offered us *double* the initial amount. I pretended to be disappointed but let them 'persuade' me to accept it and start the legal process. Inside I was yearning to shout yippee, but I kept my cool until I could ring Nigel.

"Nice one, lad," he said. My instinct had paid off. It had taken guts but, when we analysed it later, we knew in our heart of hearts that, if we had taken the first offer, the buyers would have thought we were too keen to sell. They may have thought that they were overpaying, that we lacked confidence in the business, or that there was something hidden in a closet that would bite them later.

When it comes to buying anything, always challenge the price and then **shut up**. Let the other person talk and sit in silence for as long as you have to. The old saying, 'He who speaks first, loses' is true.

This approach was further proven years later when Nigel wanted to sell part of his shareholding in our cash machine business. Our stockbrokers were desperate for shares and asked me to ask Nigel if he would sell some. I already knew that Nigel wanted to realise some cash, but I wanted to ensure that I was getting the best deal for him. Initially, they offered 50p per share, which I rejected on Nigel's behalf. The brokers then increased this offer to 62p per share, a level at which Nigel stood to receive a fairly sizeable cheque. But I rejected the offer a second time and slammed the phone down, with Nigel getting increasingly frustrated next to me and muttering that I should just sell them.

Twenty minutes later, the broker offered 72p per share, an improvement that was worth about £50,000 to Nigel. I accepted the deal for him and within two weeks he had bought himself a new 7 series BMW and a new car for his wife, for cash. *Never accept the first offer*, as nobody ever makes their best offer first. Since then, Nigel has not questioned our wisdom of never accepting the first offer.

Get upgraded

You only need 12 words to be upgraded in a hotel.

Here's what *not* to do – when you check into a hotel, don't ask whether there's a chance of an upgrade, as the staff are pre-programmed to say, "No, sorry, we are really busy" or whatever. It doesn't work.

Instead you need to use the exact phrase: "Can I ask you please, have you given me a *nice* room?" What people don't appreciate is that the person working on reception may have worked there for many years and will know which rooms are the nicest ones, which are next to the lifts, are really noisy or get the smells from the kitchen. They know that if they put you in one of those rooms, in the morning when you checkout you are not going to be happy. So, when you say the magic words, "Can I ask you please, have you given me a nice room?", they will most likely look on the screen and either say yes, I have given you a nice room, or they will say actually maybe I could give you a better room. Trust me, it works. I have been upgraded dozens of times simply by using this phrase.

Invest to accumulate

I've always been intrigued by people who make money from cars. I've met dozens of people who have told me that they managed to buy their new car below list price, run it for two years, and sell at a profit. I've never even come close to this. I've only ever paid top price, spent a fortune on servicing and completely lost my shirt when I've sold the thing. I've tried buying cars brand new at launch, cars which are rarer than most and ones that are about to have an upgrade – it's never worked. Every time my wife mentions swapping her car, I develop a foul mood and am generally grumpy.

How does the above help me to make money and become more successful? Well, I've applied the negative lessons I've learned from cars to my rules appreciating an asset that has truly performed, almost globally, for the past couple of decades. That asset is property.

A clever banker once told me that he couldn't think of a wealthy, successful client that didn't invest in property. Most wealthy individuals, he said, have a holiday home in Spain or Switzerland, and most owned their offices and factories. He even introduced me to a successful car dealer who explained that he considered himself to be running two businesses; one was selling cars and the other was his property portfolio, which happened to be the car dealerships' buildings. When car sales flagged, he said, he would consolidate and sell off sites for development. Basically, the car sales provided the cash flow to invest in the property, which increased naturally over time in any event.

You can add a property angle into your success. If you're just starting out and need premises but can't afford the deposit to buy, only take out a short lease and ensure that your business can be relocated and still thrive. Try to negotiate a right to buy the property at some point in the future.

Don't build up a fantastic sandwich shop in a busy parade of shops where you've rented, and then relocate it to a business park just because you can buy. Instead, consider if you could build your business differently, perhaps by delivering sandwiches from the business park. Similarly, if you are already tied into a long lease, or are about to take one out because it is unavoidable in the location you require, use the profits you generate to invest in another property.

If you make £20,000 and buy a new car, the following year it will only be worth £14,000 (or £9,000 if you're like me). But, if you use that £20,000 as a deposit on a house which you then let, the house will be worth £22,000 the following year. Within seven years, your deposit might well be worth £40,000 *and* the tenant will have paid five years of your mortgage, meaning your £20,000 has become £50,000. Better still, you've done relatively little. Although, if you have the time to buy run-down property and add value by doing it up, you can see even greater gains.

Early on, I had a bizarre board meeting at Cardpoint. At the time, we were still operating from a pre-war fire station that my father and I had bought for £52,500 in 1992. We were bursting at the seams and needed to move. My brother Nigel had found a perfect building under construction near Blackpool Airport, which was for sale freehold. The builder also offered to lease it to us.

We did the maths and realised that we could buy it for the same amount as if we leased it for five years at £100,000 per year. It was therefore a no-brainer to buy it as, if we did, then at the end of five years: we'd own the building, it would probably be worth £750,000 to £1m, and we'd have nothing further to pay and could stay in it forever. But, if we leased it, at the end of five years: we'd have spent £500,000, we'd have nothing to show for our £500,000, and we'd need to enter into a new lease, which would be more than £100,000 per year as, by then, we would be renting a building worth £750,000 to £1m.

Despite the obvious benefit to buying it, the board suggested we lease it instead. Their justification was that, as a publicly listed company, the City would not want us to invest in property. I argued that it wasn't an investment, just good sense, but I was shouted down and even told, "Well, entrepreneurs always think like that. We're a cash machine company, not a property company."

I immediately shut up. Then I offered to buy the building myself and lease it to Cardpoint, at arm's length, using different solicitors, independent valuers and a different bank. The other directors agreed and Cardpoint paid £90,000 plus VAT per year to rent the building – it's now valued at £1.04m. Thank you very much.

Don't blow it

As a general rule, people who make money very quickly don't tend to hold onto it for long. Many people who win the lottery start off in a three-bed semi, win £5m and, five years later, are still in the three-bed semi with no money left simply because they didn't know how to adjust to having money or how to manage it wisely.

I was lucky in many ways. Because it took me a long time to make any proper money, once I had it I was determined not to let it go. If you come into a large sum of money very suddenly, take your time to understand how to handle it. Don't throw it around or rush into anything. And if you sell your business for a large sum of money, remember all the long hours you put into making it a success and proceed with great care.

Stay humble

When I arrived home, having received an offer for Cardpoint, I went to the kitchen and immediately said to my wife, Angela, "I appreciate that you have done most of the work for the last seven years with the children and our home and I want you to know how grateful I am. I know I have worked thousands of hours and have barely seen you, and you've done thousands of school runs, looked after our home and supported me unconditionally, but it will have been worth it. It's all going to pay off now. I have reached the point where we have 300 staff, 6,500 machines and are dispensing over £500m each month across three countries. I have had an offer for the business, valuing it at £170m."

Angela looked straight at me and I could feel my heart beating in my chest. I genuinely knew that she was about to say something profound about my success and achievements, how clever I was, how glad she was that she had picked me out of all the men in the world she could have chosen, how the sacrifices had all been worth it and how proud she was of me.

Angela turned and walked towards the window and looked into the garden. I'll never forget her words when she said, "It looks like it's going to rain, will you bring the washing in?"

As I unpegged the washing, I realised that however clever I thought I was, if the washing needs to be brought in, nothing else really matters. I chuckled to myself and when I went back into the kitchen, wet from the rain, carrying shirts, socks and underpants, I kissed Angela and said, "Thank you. Thank you for not letting me get ahead of myself!" Angela smiled at me and said, "I know you're good, but I wouldn't want it to go to your head. And besides, the bins need to go out…"

Life after Cardpoint

After leaving Cardpoint, I began to look for something else to do.

My brother Nigel and I had decided to go our own ways. We had worked together for about 18 years and had literally never had a cross word, but we both fancied a change. Nigel had been an excellent business partner, right-hand man, confidant. Most of all, he'd been a good laugh. I do admit to giving him a bit of a hard time sometimes, but he did the same with me and that's probably why it worked – we were always (brutally) honest with each other. Since then, we have been more like brothers again, which has been great.

My insurance broker Curtis Dowman told me that the stock of bungalows was declining every year because the number being built was less than the number being demolished, or built on to add a second storey. Having always been obsessed with business models, my plan became to buy bungalows, renovate them and rent them out with the logo, 'Our bungalows, Your home'. I was hooked.

It worked an absolute treat. I bought 14 bungalows to rent out and then bought a piece of land to build another 12 bungalows on. I sold the latter as a package to a Housing Association, at less than I could have achieved, because it was helpful to house people who needed to live on one floor. I bought all my bungalows in or around Blackpool because many people who come to Blackpool for their holidays want to move here when they retire. From a business model perspective, it was perfect. I showed this plan to my bank manager, who burst out laughing and said: "Millsy, you are the only person I know who would write a business plan for buying buy-to-let properties. Everyone else just buys them and gives them to an agent to deal with."

Amongst other things, I had figured out a great way to buy bungalows. With the odd exception, I only viewed bungalows that were marketed as 'vacant possession'. As many older people live in bungalows, it tends to mean that the person has passed away and the bungalow is in probate. Most families, as sad as they are about their mum or dad passing away, just seem to want the money quickly.

I know this for two reasons. First, I have viewed bungalows where there is half a cup of tea and a slice of toast with a bite out of it on the table. On that viewing, I wondered whether if I had felt the bed it would have still been warm. Second, I always chat to the estate agent and find out about the probate, such as how many brothers and sisters stand to inherit. This is because (using easy figures), if the bungalow is for sale at £100,000 and there are three of them, they stand to receive £33,333 each.

The secret is to offer an amount which is easily divisible by the number of inheritors. In the example, I would offer £90,000, meaning that the three would receive £30,000 each. To be honest though, the next easily divisible number below £100,000 is £75,000 and I would start at that. This tactic works because, instead of focusing on the £25,000 reduction (from £100,000 to £75,000), people tend to look at the fact that they will receive £25,000 rather than £33,000 each – only a £8,000 reduction.

Also, I always put the offer in writing, outlining all of mine and my solicitor's details, a time frame for exchange and completion and so on. This makes my offer very compelling, as it emphasises the certainty of the transaction if they withdraw the property from sale and tempts the siblings into taking the quick, certain money, as opposed to a drawn-out affair.

If this seems a bit ruthless, rest assured I have seen inheritors acting worse. In one instance, when I arrived to pick up the keys of a property, two brothers and a sister were having a three-way, tug-of-war over a dining table left on the driveway. I thought I was going to have to call the police.

I was very happy investing in bungalows, but my bank manager told me that he thought commercial property was a better bet because it offered better covenants and a higher quality of portfolio. So, stupidly and against my intuition, I listened to him and began to buy shops, offices and land instead of bungalows.

The idea was to buy shops, install a cash machine and then rent them out to retailers. The shop would be more appealing for having the cash machine, and I would receive all of that income, as I wouldn't have to give the retailer a cut. To generate further income, I would rent the flat above to a tenant, which was good for security as there would be someone there 24/7.

I remembered that our most profitable machine at Cardpoint had been inherited through the HBOS acquisition and was in a shop in Edinburgh. It was a tiny shop, with basically just the cash machine in it, so we only paid £5,000 a year in rent and yet the cash machine made £100,000 a year.

Where I went wrong was that instead of staying local, as I had with my bungalows, I started buying shops all over the country. Yet deep down I knew that the secret to owning property was to have it within half an hour of your home, so that you can easily deal with any problems that arise. In my enthusiasm to build up a portfolio, I bought shops everywhere, thinking that it would be easy.

It wasn't and the situation quickly turned into a nightmare. For one, if a shop in Nottingham had a broken pipe that needed fixing, I wouldn't know any plumbers in Nottingham and so would have to try and find one or somehow deal with it myself. The other problem was that we were heading into a recession and I realised that having cash machines that charged a fee was perhaps not a good idea anymore. After acquiring 25 shops, I got rid of the ones that were located far away or working at a loss, and just held onto the few that were local.

Even those occasionally bought headaches though. One day I received a call saying that there was a flood in one of my shops which was coming from the flat above. I quickly drove round and, because I owned the whole block, let myself into the basement to shut off the water for all four shops and eight flats. But the water continued to gush into the shop, so I knocked on the door of the flat above it. There was no answer, so I borrowed a ladder from a builder working across the road and climbed up to peer into the window on the first floor.

Oddly, the windows were open but the curtains were closed, and the windows had been boarded up and painted black. Fearing that something horrible might have happened, I called the police and, when they broke into the flat, they discovered that the tenants had built a cannabis farm inside. It was like something from a film.

One of the policemen asked if I would provide a statement, so we went to sit in his police van outside the flat. Suddenly, a procession of everyone I had ever known seemed to appear to find me sitting in a police van looking as though I had done something terrible. There were people tapping on the window, people both from school and business, saying, "Hello Mark, what have you been doing?" It felt as though half my family had turned up too.

In the end, a guy popped up saying he was from the local

newspaper, the *Evening Gazette*, and was looking for the landlord. By now I was completely fed up with the unwanted attention and told the journalist I had never heard of the landlord. Then I raced home as fast as I could.

The story made the front page of the *Evening Gazette*, but fortunately it didn't have my name in it or my photo. I quickly revised my views on publicity and decided that not *all* publicity was good publicity.

Meanwhile, a lot of people were getting in contact with me to find out more about my experiences at Cardpoint and how I had managed to start a business that had become so successful. I was more than willing to share my knowledge and so started being invited to speak about my experiences at business clubs, conferences and events.

The first paid speech I made was a disaster. I was asked to talk at a stationery wholesalers conference in Birmingham, so I agreed to a fee of £1,000 and wrote a very funny speech. But just as I was about to go on stage, the organiser rushed up to me and asked if I would talk about the impact of the internet on retail stationery instead. I initially said no, but he begged me, saying that it would really help him if I could do that. I reluctantly agreed and quickly wrote some more slides while I was literally standing at the lectern.

The first part of my speech went well, but as soon as I deviated from what I had planned, I completely died because I didn't really know what I was talking about. I never really recovered. At the end the organiser came up to me, shook my hand weakly and said, "It didn't go as well as we had hoped, did it?" I was furious, not just with him, but also with myself for not insisting on making the speech I had wanted to make.

Ever since then I have always made the same speech. It's funny, motivational, informative and people like it, so I really can't see the point of changing it. When I was asked to speak at an accountancy conference in Miami, I listened carefully to the company chairman talking about all the messages he wanted me to weave in, the little plugs for business, the digs about competitors and so on. At the end of the meeting, he left and I asked the guy who was arranging it if they had a bin. He pointed to one in the corner of the room, I ripped up my notes and put them in, telling him that I had one speech and it would do the trick.

On the day in Miami, the guy who arranged it was really nervous. I asked him if he was speaking, because I had only ever seen somebody like that when they were going on stage, but he said, "No, I'm just nervous because you are going on."

Despite his fears, my speech went incredibly well, apart from the odd joke. As it was an international conference of accountants, most people were wearing headsets and there was a bank of translators at the back of the room, translating the speeches in real time.

This meant that as I delivered punchlines, the English speakers would laugh first, then it was a race for the French, Mandarin, Spanish, Greek, Portuguese, Korean and other translators to deliver my jokes as well as they could. This meant the laughter came in waves, as each group was delivered the joke, which made the whole event even funnier. At one point, the Korean translator got the giggles at a joke and could barely translate. That set the Koreans off, who never actually heard the end of the speech and just laughed throughout.

All speaking events have their moments. At Merrill Lynch in London, I followed a speaker talking very dryly about tax and most of the audience seemed to be asleep. I pointed this out when I stood up and soon had everyone doing star jumps on the spot, "To make sure they had enough blood pumping through their veins to keep them awake during my speech." It turned out that my less-than-subtle inference about the previous speaker being boring was taken badly and he stormed off the stage – much to the amusement of the enlivened crowd.

Doing all these speaking gigs was great fun but, rather than just talking about how businesses could grow, I realised that I wanted to see if I could actually help individual businesses be the best they could be. I started offering my services as a non-executive director, with businesses paying me a daily rate for one day a month of my time.

The first business that took me on was a manufacturing firm, which was run by an old school friend. He contacted me out of the blue to see if I would like to be non-executive chairman. The business designed, manufactured and distributed a range of goods and was run mainly out of the Far East, with a head office in the UK. When I joined it had a turnover of around $70m.

It was a really fun business to work with, largely because a lot of the board meetings were held in Hong Kong and the other board members and I would go out there to attend them. Once, we flew to Hong Kong to work in the office there for a week, but as soon as we arrived the chief executive announced that he would show us the sights instead. We spent the next five days popping into the office in the morning to show our faces and then going off to see all the best bits of Hong Kong – including long alcoholic lunches in the best restaurants and drinks in the Hong Kong Press Club.

We got back to the UK on the Saturday morning, absolutely exhausted and having done the minimal amount of work. When I rang the chief executive on the Monday to ask him how everything was going, he said, "I can't speak now, Millsy, I'm on the way to Hong Kong to do all the work we should have done last week."

I soon realised that the business was being run in a very different way to how I had run Cardpoint. The senior managers of the business were obsessed with making as much profit as they could. They wanted to charge customers as much as they could and were keen to squeeze the suppliers as hard as they could. Least important to them, in my opinion, was anyone who worked for them, who they tried to pay as little as possible.

The culture was very different too. The chief executive was fairly tyrannical and one day he decided to ban the use of the internet in the business simply because he had found somebody reading the newspaper online at lunchtime while they were eating a sandwich at their desk. When someone announced that one of the women in the accounts department was pregnant, the first response from one member of the board was to ask if we could sack her – I had been about to suggest that we buy her some flowers to congratulate her. The board member later told me that he was just joking about sacking her, but I was never 100% sure.

Despite the fun times, I realised that the business wasn't a good fit for me culturally, because I had always run my businesses in a completely different way: look after your staff, look after your suppliers, look after your customers and try to do a better deal for them, and *then* the money will flow. I'd learnt very early on that if you chase the money it doesn't come. We parted company amicably and are still friends.

I also realised that my own personal business model was flawed. In 2010, we were visiting some friends in Tenerife when the Icelandic volcano erupted on the last day of our holiday. The resulting ash cloud grounded all flights. We were stuck on the island and, although our hotel continued to provide us with a room and meals because we had booked a package holiday, it really wasn't the same knowing that we couldn't leave even if we wanted to.

For the first 13 days of our holiday we had been happily lying by the pool while the kids played in it, with my wife saying, "This place is like paradise, the sun never stops shining, we are having a great time, it's like heaven on earth." Come day 17, however, not knowing if we would ever be able to leave and see home again, my wife was shouting, "Get me off this bloody hellhole" and I'm thinking, hang on a minute, four days ago it was paradise.

For me there was an even bigger problem. My various board meetings were due to take place the following week, and now I was going to miss them because I was stuck in Tenerife unable to fly home. I was also going to miss several meetings with businesses that I was doing advisory work for. The problem was that in the business model I had set up for myself, all the work I was doing was on a pay-per-day basis – so if I didn't turn up in person to these meetings, I wasn't going to be paid. Therefore, being stuck in Tenerife was not only annoying, but it ended up being extremely costly. Yes, I had a great tan, but I had also lost out on a significant amount of earnings.

It was a real low point in my life. I realised that, ever since leaving Cardpoint, I had basically just been scrabbling around working for people on a daily rate. I didn't really want to have my own business again and I quite liked helping people with their businesses, but then they would just say, yes that was good and cut me adrift when they felt they didn't need me anymore. I would think, well, hang on, I added a load of value there and was paid a pittance. I didn't even receive any recognition or sense of achievement, so what's the point?

I talked it through with my wife and she said, "Well, you go into businesses and reinvent their business models, so why don't you reinvent your own business model of being a non-exec?" I thought, she's right. How can I teach people a better model for their business when my own business model was rubbish? Then I thought it through some more and realised that I needed to completely reinvent my non-executive role. I had a huge amount of knowledge and experience to share, but right now it was being wasted.

Forget about being a non-exec; I was going to become a *super* non-exec instead.

I started to become excited about my new plan. As a super non-exec, I could be given specific goals to achieve and be rewarded for delivering them. That might be selling the business outright, bringing in private-equity investors, or floating the business on the stock exchange. I would be paid a monthly retainer, regardless of whether I was physically there or not, plus a share of any upside that I had helped to achieve. If the aim was to sell the business, for example, then I would receive a share of any price we achieved above the amount the owner had expected to get without my help.

The business owners would be happy because they would be getting specific, measurable outcomes, and I would be happy because I would have a far more interesting and rewarding role than simply turning up for a board meeting once a month. And I would receive a share of the upside in return for my hard work, rather than spending my time worrying about whether I could get to a board meeting or not.

It was definitely a eureka moment.

My GOLDEN RULES for getting through tough times

Your best weapon is your intuition

Start listening to your instinct. My intuition told me that the bungalows were – and are – a great investment opportunity, but others convinced me that the grass was greener in commercial property. I should have listened to myself, not them.

Embrace your mistakes

No matter how clever you are, you really learn by trying and making mistakes, because it is only then that the lesson tends to stick with you. Will I buy commercial property again? Only if it instinctively feels right, if the return is demonstrably better than that provided from my residential portfolio.

Keep it in perspective

Losing money is not the end of the world. Business is competitive and it is not realistic to expect to never lose money. In fact, if I could guarantee that everything I bought would go up in value, there would be no challenge, fun, foresight or edge required. Every time you make a loss, you're one step closer to making a fortune.

Becoming a Super Non-Exec

ired up by my new strategy, I started looking around for an opportunity to put it into practice. To do this, I needed to look for a business that might be interested in taking me on as a super non-exec.

Hurst

My first attempt was with Hurst Accountants, who I joined as a chairman on a super non-exec arrangement.

The role itself went well. One of the first things I did was to persuade them to have a pink logo because I felt they needed to stand out more. When the marketing director proposed the idea at a board meeting, only I agreed with him, but by the end of the meeting we had managed to persuade everyone that they needed to do this. The bright pink logo transformed their business, which has since become very successful.

I also persuaded them to rethink their pitch to potential clients. They usually pitched to the CEO and the financial director of a business, telling this story about how they had once gone in to do an audit and had uncovered a massive fraud that had been going on for years, but which the senior directors knew nothing about. As a result of the investigation, a lot of people got sacked at the business and, even though the financial director wasn't in on the fraud, he lost his job too because it happened on his watch.

Hurst were extremely proud of this achievement because it showed that they had found something other auditors had missed. The problem was that every time they told the story, I could see the financial director to whom they were pitching thinking, 'Hang on a minute, so if this lot come in here and discover some kind of fraudulent activity, then I could end up getting fired because I didn't know anything about it.' After the pitch, the CEO would almost definitely ask the financial director what they thought of Hurst and it would be far too easy for the financial director to say that they didn't like them.

I suggested to Hurst that they might want to start leaving this story out because they were alienating 50% of their audience every time they told it. They changed their pitch after that.

The bigger problem for me personally was that the accountancy firm had been set up as a limited liability partnership, rather than a private limited company or publicly listed company. This meant that there was no straightforward way for them to give me equity in the business, a key element of my super non-exec strategy. They initially discussed giving me equity after two years of working with them, but this was pushed back each year until, after five years, I still had no equity. I decided it was time to move on.

It was a lesson learned. But on the upside, it has always been good for my CV, as I have been able to say that I was the chairman of an accountancy firm for five years, something which tells people that I understand accounts. They were also nice people to work with and I am still in touch with them.

Tactical Solutions

My involvement with Tactical Solutions, a business that provided outsourced sales teams for Heinz and other big brands, was much more successful. Owned by Lorna Davidson, the business was clearly different from the outset.

I had known Lorna for a few years through a business club and, when she agreed to take me on as a super non-exec, she agreed to pay me £6,000 a month – six times as much as the £1,000 she was paying her current non-exec. I had a good look at her business and told her I thought it was worth £20m. Lorna was a bit taken aback as she had started the business in her garden shed with nothing but a mobile phone and, at first, she didn't seem to appreciate the value she had built. I pointed out everything she had achieved and how great the business was, and we agreed that I would take a percentage of anything we sold it for over £20m. Lorna's downside was minimal and, when she agreed, I had a warm feeling that my new business model would work.

At the first board meeting it became clear that Lorna had created a fantastic business. Normally a board meeting starts with a report by the CEO, followed by a report by the financial director. Yet here, the conversation was all about what the company could do to give its employees a better experience, how they could pay them more and give them more time off to achieve a better work-life balance. Secondly, what could the company do to provide a better experience for their customers – could they charge them less and do more? And thirdly, were they paying their suppliers enough? Could they pay them more to ensure they were doing a good job?

Only at the end of the board meeting did they start to discuss the financial numbers. Lorna explained that the business was making a decent profit because staff loved the business and were happy to work overtime for free, customers loved the company and were asking if they could do more business, and suppliers said they loved dealing with the company. However, Lorna felt it could do much, much more. All the way through I was thinking, 'Well that, my friend, is how to run a business.' But on the other hand, it needed to move up a number of gears if we were really going to achieve a significant sum for it.

I knew that both my super non-exec role and my programme for improving the business would take hard work and determination in order to achieve a trade sale. So I set about really pushing the entire business along.

Lorna had embraced the whole super non-exec concept and reported very early on that I gave her a better perspective on her business just by looking at it as somebody who had worked in lots of different businesses. Also, she appreciated that I questioned everything and never let her off the hook for actions we had agreed to take.

Tactical Solutions was already in good shape, but we needed to work on professionalising the business across the board. To do this, we needed to grind out the numbers, which we achieved through drawing up an incredibly detailed and granular business plan. This included many elements Lorna had never really put down on paper before, although most of them she had already thought about. In this way, I brought the discipline of putting everything into a fully formed plan and holding everybody to it, whilst keeping an eye out for left-field opportunities too.

After I had done just two months work with Lorna, she was so impressed with the difference I had made that she asked if I could double my days in return for £12,000 a month – an offer I duly accepted.

It was now clear that this arrangement was going to work.

As part of my super non-exec programme, I insisted upon administration of the business becoming more formalised. While Lorna liked structure, it was proving hard to instil in others and, as a result, the business's structure was demonstrably lax. In response, we ensured that, going forward, the scheduling of board meetings and actions points were documented and met, and that staff were held to account for their targets. These were all things that needed to be entrenched within the company if it were to continue to prosper.

Also introduced were a host of key performance indicators, which measured people's progress and output. We started with consolidating job roles and responsibilities, then moved on to resetting targets and revising reward structures for high-performing individuals. By driving our staff each week towards measurable goals, the whole business started to function better and achieve more in less time.

As a disciplinarian myself, I can safely say that the strategy of holding people, even a business owner, to account works – just be clear about your expectations and people will, for the most part, aim to meet them.

Part of this approach relies upon the fact that Lorna, like me, was prepared to be tough on people, as well as to motivate them. While this did mean that some staff left, we were sure that their departure was best for both parties.

It may seem odd that I was ordering the owner around, but that was a requirement of the job. Lorna had built the business at a certain pace and she demanded that I push her on the finances, action points and how she dealt with her team. The result was a newly motivated Lorna, who was an unstoppable force. Simply through being more disciplined and ruthless in the execution of her plan, everything stepped up a gear. Indeed, my intervention only accelerated the inevitable.

Tactical Solutions had 500 salespeople who would go into

supermarkets across the country to offer promotional deals on behalf of the brands they represented. They would then monitor the sales data going through the tills to record the improvement in sales.

What made the business model so clever was that each time salespeople would only go to 90% of the supermarkets in the country. In this way, Tactical Solutions could clearly show the impact that their activity had on sales as compared with the 10% of supermarkets they did not engage with. If the brand was running a massive television campaign at the same time, for example, no one could ever say, well the rise in sales was because of that. As a result, they were able to show that for every £1 Heinz spent with them, for instance, they received something like £2.74 back in sales.

In one board meeting, I asked when was the last time that a board member had spent a day with one of the sales team to see how it actually worked in practice. Everyone suddenly became very interested in looking at their feet when it turned out that no one had ever done this before. So I asked Lorna if she could arrange for me to go out on the road.

Lorna fixed me up with a salesperson to follow around on a day when the sales team had been given a promotion to sell on behalf of a wholesaler, involving chocolate and Coca-Cola in convenience stores rather than supermarkets. If a store placed an order for a minimum amount of a certain brand of chocolates they would also receive a free case of Coca-Cola.

I watched as the woman I was shadowing tried to sell the promotion in two stores. Neither of them took the deal, so I did the math and suggested that she offer the promotion the other way round: instead of trying to sell the chocolates and give away the Coca-Cola, I suggested that she sell the Coca-Cola and give the chocolates away for free.

Doing it this way round would make the retailer more comfortable about saying yes because, due to the popularity of Coca-Cola, they knew they would be able to sell it – the free chocolate would simply be a bonus. When we arrived at the next convenience store, the salesperson pitched it this way round and the guy promptly signed up. She couldn't believe it and immediately wanted to share the news with the rest of the team. Tactical Solutions had a system whereby one person could leave a voice message for all the other salespeople, so she quickly left a voicemail telling everyone to promote the deal in the new way we had devised.

By the afternoon, the salespeople were managing to sign up nearly every store they visited and sales sharply increased. Over the next few days orders continued to come in, with retailers asking how much quantity they could have, and by the end of the promotion, sales were ten times the number they had been expecting. The boss of the chocolate firm told Lorna that he couldn't believe they had been able to achieve such a fantastic outcome.

Alongside that, we did some Heinz work and I really threw myself into my role. That evening, when I returned home from work my wife Angela asked what I had been doing that day. I told her that I had been stacking cans of baked beans onto shelves in a Tesco supermarket. Angela laughed and said she had hoped my career had progressed beyond shelf-stacking by now.

Lorna used to laugh her socks off because in the two and a half years I worked with her, although I only ever did that one day out with the sales team, I always discussed sales as though I was an absolute expert. Whenever we discussed the sales process for the business I was talking about, it was as though I had been a Tactical Solution's salesman for the last ten years.

Lorna also wanted to look at how we could make the sales team more profitable. So, together we embarked upon an exercise of scrutinising every customer contract, to look at profit margins, contribution in terms of actual revenue, and cost to the company. Equally, we discussed what was happening in the market, where customers were saturated with our services and where there were new opportunities to be taken. Lastly, we charted what our cost base would look like when we expanded and the effect this would have on our short- and long-term profitability.

For the first time, we really analysed Lorna's competition, spending hours trying to determine how they differentiated from us, what we could do to win work from them and how we could outsell them. During this time, I attended various customer pitches, as well as staff meetings, sales conferences and dealings with suppliers – with my reputation as a hard task manager seeming to precede me, our people began to up their game. We were winning work because our prices were even more competitive now that we knew exactly how much our execution costs were. And with a stable cost base and a team who would meet and beat all expectations, we were able to consistently generate profit.

With 500 salespeople, I knew that any actions taken by the team would have a discernible, positive impact – not least to the services offered by Tactical Solutions and its bottom line. We initially thought about selling advertising on cars, as our people spent a lot of time on the road driving from supermarket to supermarket. But we rejected that idea because many of the sales force were graduates and had a tendency to crash their cars… a lot.

Our next idea was to find a new category of product that the sales team could sell alongside baked beans, chocolate and so on. All of

Tactical Solutions' competitors were chasing the most popular brands though, so we were keen to find a product category that had been overlooked.

In search of inspiration, Lorna and I visited a supermarket together, where we realised that although the pet food aisle was huge and clearly a massive seller, it was also really disorganised. We knew that Mars owned several pet food brands, including Pedigree Chum, so we sent them a proposal and they signed us up. Suddenly our sales force were twice as efficient, because they had pet food to sell as well as their other products.

Another matter that I felt we needed to address was Lorna's occasional lack of self-confidence. Whilst she had undoubtedly built a great business, it was clear that the preceding ten years of rough and tumble had taken its toll. To correct this, I constantly recited Lorna's success back to her, demonstrated that when she took action it produced an incredible outcome, and just generally kept her on course by reaffirming her belief in herself.

Besides this, I kept Lorna very focused on her end goal, to sell Tactical Solutions, and her own role. Entrepreneurs always have new ideas, but it was my job to be tough on Lorna and make sure she kept to her original plan. We had some unpleasant moments, but any heated words were soon replaced with laughter.

My programme for selling a business brought great benefits to Lorna and the Tactical Solutions team though. Consisting of logical steps to be undertaken in a timely manner, it leads to a well-prepared business. This invariably adds value to the company, as both owner and business are prepared for the sale – a process which can be daunting to those who have not sold before.

This meant that when we offered Tactical Solutions for sale, the company was thriving, it was an enjoyable place to work and Lorna had a comprehensive understanding of the business. Countless hours spent questioning every aspect of the business and refining the important elements with complete focus had undoubtedly paid off.

Lorna and I did the presentation to each buyer together, which aimed to outline all the points of interest within the business. We used graphics and charts, and structured the presentation with a powerful opening, informative middle and compelling end. Besides this, we had the presentation professionally printed and had rehearsed the speech intensively to ensure that we were word perfect. The presentation flowed, and everybody complimented us on its professionalism and thoroughness. Ultimately, the presentation generated great excitement about Tactical Solutions and potential buyers were all extremely keen to learn more.

Ironically, Lorna and I presented the business so well that most potential buyers asked why we were selling it! Fortunately, we had rehearsed an answer for this and Lorna was able to state that she believed Tactical Solutions was ready to become a part of a bigger organisation and that that was Lorna's dream for it.

Part of the presentation's challenge, however, was to not reveal *too much* information, since not everyone would be successful in their bid. We therefore endeavoured to keep some pieces of information to ourselves, only hinting at their existence, which actually helped to increase the already strong interest.

Initial bids started at £20m.

Lorna was absolutely staggered by these opening offers. Even though I had told her right from the start that the business was worth this amount, she had never really believed me until she saw the numbers in black and white.

From my perspective though, this outcome was the inevitable

conclusion to all of our hard work. After instilling a formal business structure, ruthlessly examining our finances and constantly motivating our teams to beat targets, Tactical Solutions had finally become the market-leading, field services business it was destined to be. Following my professional programme had undoubtedly transformed the foundations of Lorna's business. Lorna herself had also evolved under my guidance, turning into a powerful, self-confident and dynamic leader.

With several interested buyers bidding for the company, we managed to push the price up to £29m. I called Lorna and said I thought we could get the price up to £30m, but she decided that £29m was enough. In fact, it was way over her expectations and a fantastic result. When asked why she didn't want to hold out for £30m, Lorna simply said she'd tell me later.

We agreed to sell the business for £29m to St Ives plc, a listed company that had made its fortune by printing titles such as the Harry Potter series and *The Economist*. I knew that St Ives plc would end up buying us because, during our presentation to them, they had showed us their strategy document, which listed Tactical Solutions as one of four acquisitions they intended to make. I think they'd already told their investors that Tactical Solutions was in the bag and that they were definitely buying us.

On the morning of the sale, Lorna handed me a cheque. She told me that it wouldn't clear the bank unless we signed the deal, but that she wanted me to have my money first as a reward for the discipline, professionalism and enthusiasm I had shown throughout my time working at Tactical Solutions, which I was really touched by. I immediately put the cheque in my car for safekeeping – I didn't want to lose it if I ended up getting drunk later.

Our buyers wanted to complete the deal by 4.30pm, in order for them to be able to announce it on the stock market before it closed. This worked to our advantage and we managed to secure every concession we'd wanted simply because the other side were up against the clock and had no choice but to agree. By the end of the process, the guy would have signed over his grandmother just to get the deal done in time.

By 4.31pm, we were celebrating the deal with a glass of champagne and our team of advisors. They were all clearly in for a big night but, after a couple of hours, I realised I was just too tired to continue. Lorna and I had been working on this deal solidly for six months and I was absolutely exhausted. Lorna was too, so the two of us left and went home.

The next morning, I rang Lorna at home and her husband, Geoff, answered. I asked him how he felt and he said: "To be honest, Mark, we liked the business so much, it feels like we've sold one of the kids." I laughed and replied, "But Geoff, you wouldn't have got as much for one of the kids." Fortunately, he laughed too.

He put Lorna on the phone and she said, "I got home, kissed Geoff and the kids, had baked beans on toast and cried my eyes out. But I checked my bank account this morning and, I have to say, I'm not crying anymore."

Lorna kindly repeated how much I had helped her and Tactical Solutions. She went on to say that whenever asked, in years to come, for the ways in which I had helped her to improve, prepare and sell her business, that she would have to apologise for how long the list would be.

It was a great way to finish a deal, to know that I had brought real value and was appreciated for doing so. Lorna did add that I was the toughest and fairest 'boss' she had ever worked for, which I took as a great compliment.

Lastly, I asked Lorna why she had been so insistent that we sell the business for £29m rather than hold out for £30m. She told me that before I had joined the business, she had been offered £2.5m for the whole thing. When she told the buyer that she would agree to the deal if he raised the price to £3m, he walked away. This time, Lorna didn't want to wreck the deal for the sake of £1m, and she hadn't wanted to tell me about the £2.5m offer in case I decided that the business was actually only worth that amount. Lorna had had nothing to fear though, as I always knew it was worth a fortune.

As my share of the deal was quite a bit bigger than my previous daily rate, I knew that my first super non-exec role had been a spectacular success.

Violet – women board members

The board of Tactical Solutions had been mostly made up of women, something that was fairly unusual in the business world, and it gave me an idea. While I was still chairman of the company, I decided to start up a business to help women become non-executive directors. I knew that there were many highly capable and experienced women in business, but that they often lacked the knowledge, contacts and even self-confidence to apply for non-executive roles. My plan was to run training courses to show women how to do it.

I called my business Violet, because I decided that if someone wanted to be a female non-exec director then they couldn't be a shrinking violet. I sat at my desk one evening and created a website, www.violet.uk.com. The landing page read:

"I have contacted the big head-hunters to find them patronising and who, even despite all of my experience, made me feel as though I was wasting their time. I can see how I can add value to companies as a non-executive director but cannot seem to generate the opportunity. I just keep hearing that I don't have a chance yet, in my heart, I know I have a great deal to offer." As said by far, far too many qualified, intelligent and experienced women who contact Mark Mills every day.

The website went live in February 2011 and straightaway I received hundreds of enquiries. I therefore decided to meet each candidate in person before accepting them onto my course.

One of the very first women I met with, a successful lawyer in London, turned out to be the wife of the editor of the *Sunday Times* newspaper. Within days, I received a call from a *Sunday Times* journalist who was writing a feature on women board members. When the article was published, the number of enquiries shot up. Ironically, the woman never signed up for the course, but the piece really helped to spread the word.

I charged £3,000 for a six-month training course – consisting of one session each month – and ran them for groups of 10–20 women at a time. The course covered everything from how the non-exec director role works and how to act in a board meeting, to how to be resilient and how to interview well.

I knew from experience that if a woman is an eight out of ten in terms of being suitable for a role, she will offer evidence of being a five or six in an interview and hope that the interviewing panel will join the dots. Whereas, if a man is an eight out of ten, he will say he is a nine and a half. This makes any decision to appoint a man over a woman an easy one, as the man will have said at the interview that he can do things that the woman seemingly can't.

These courses initially worked really well. I even started getting enquiries from companies who wanted to appoint female non-executive directors, so I managed to place 24 women in roles. However, even if it did tend to improve the prospects of the women who completed the course, Violet was not as successful as I would have liked. I think this was partly due to many women not possessing the confidence to pay to learn.

And as my next company, Violet had a lousy business model, which ended up costing me money. I didn't mind though, because I felt that I was helping others and giving back to the business community. It was clear that it was never going to be a large business though, so I stopped running courses and just kept it going to help women individually if they contacted me.

My GOLDEN RULES for becoming a super non-exec

Decide right at the start how much the business you are helping is worth

Once you start doing the work, the founder will be able to see the value increasing and therefore raise their expectations about the valuation. Nail it down at the start.

Make sure you like the people, the product and the marketplace (in that order)

If the directors you are going to work alongside don't fit with you ethically and culturally, it won't work.

Ask for equity

Make sure you receive some form of equity and that they are willing to undertake some sort of transaction. If you don't establish this and keep to the programme, you will simply end up being a non-exec for a long time for relatively little reward.

Be metronomic

I always agree to see the business owner at the same time on the same day of every week. That way, I secure my weekly slot and it's easy for everybody. Out of sight, out of mind – busy business owners soon forget who you are if you don't see them regularly and then they start to change their plans.

My Next Wins

Garside & Laycock

After giving a talk about my experience at Tactical Solutions in a business club in Harrogate, a man called Paul Garside asked me whether we could schedule a meeting. It turned out, Paul ran a construction business called Garside & Laycock, which provided facilities management and maintenance services to Royal Mail and other blue chip companies. He had a team of 100 people, who did everything from fixing broken doors to reorganising depots.

Having run Garside & Laycock for 30 years, Paul was now keen to sell the business and had been offered £3m for it – but the deal had fallen through. We arranged to visit Paul's accountants, in Preston, who told us that the market had become a bit tougher, so the business would now only be worth £2.5m.

I told Paul that I strongly disagreed with this advice.

Having taken a closer look at Paul's business, I told him I believed it to be worth £10m. We agreed that I would come in as the chairman of the business in my super non-exec arrangement, with Paul agreeing to pay me a monthly retainer and a share of any price we received for the business over £3m.

Paul was a savvy businessman though, and soon said that if we were to embark upon selling Garside & Laycock together, he wanted to alter my terms of business. I thought, 'Here we go, everyone wants to reinvent the wheel.' To my total surprise, and why Paul and I are best friends to this day, Paul wanted to increase my share of the upside. He had figured out that I didn't need the money and was helping him because I wanted to – he wanted me to 'Shoot for the moon and even if we miss, we will land amongst the stars.'

I introduced Paul to Rothschilds, who had acted for me at Cardpoint, and they agreed to take over as the company's corporate financial advisor. For the next six months, we worked really hard on getting the business in shape for a sale by addressing several issues to do with the management and customers.

But then one day Paul said that he needed to speak to me. He said the business was going so well, that he didn't think he wanted to sell it anymore. I looked at him and said, "Well, Paul, there are only two words to that." Then I swore at him. Taken aback, he said, "What do you mean?"

I said, "Paul, I am like your personal trainer at the gym. If you lose me, you will stop going to the gym and won't become fit. If you let me go, in six months both you and the business will be back to where you started. There is no way you'll be able to maintain the pace we're going at, because right now I have my hand on your back, pushing you along."

Paul paused for a moment and then said: "You're right, forget what I said. I apologise, that won't happen again." We both laughed and after that we were fine, so we got back on track.

As Paul and I frequently travelled to London to meet with potential buyers of his business, we often stayed in hotels and ate out together. One night, we went to our hotel restaurant and Paul ordered steak and chips. He took the first bite and started choking… badly.

I didn't know whether to give him the Heimlich manoeuvre, the kiss of life or just thump him on the back. I decided to go for the last option and, after I had thumped him on the back for a while, a big piece of steak shot across the table. Paul was quite shaken up, so once he'd regained his composure I said, "Paul, I'd have really missed you as a friend if you'd choked to death. But, to be honest, all I could think about was the new car I'm planning to buy with the fee I get from selling your business." This made him laugh and definitely broke the ice after his near-death experience. I didn't charge him extra for saving his life.

At work, I actively looked for ways to add value to Garside & Laycock. Before one board meeting, I started reading the company's Lost Tender report, a list of all the work it had unsuccessfully bid on. For example, the company had unsuccessfully bid £300,000 for a contract to build garages for a council in Manchester. Afterwards, the business received a report stating that the contract had been given to a firm that bid £295,000.

Paul explained that they wanted a profit margin of 20% for every piece of work they did, so would sometimes lose out to a rival who put in a lower bid.

I was confused about one thing though: whenever the business *did* win a contract for, say, £300,000, it never showed up in the accounts like this, but would instead appear as a £350,000 contract. Paul explained that whenever they turned up to do a job, they would invariably be asked to do additional work, which would be paid for via a change order. On a £300,000 contract, for example, they would typically pick up extra work of £50,000. This was great for business because, as the workers were already on site, a profit margin of around 50% would be made on the additional work.

I looked at Paul and said, "Hang on a minute, if you are making a 20% profit margin on the £300,000, and a 50% profit margin on the extra £50,000, your overall profit margin is 24%. So why not bid about 2% lower for all the work you pitch for? By doing this, you will be more likely to win the contract, and the higher profit margin from the additional work will make up for the slightly lower profit margin on the main piece of work. For instance, if you bid £294,000 instead of your normal £300,000, and then pick up an additional £50,000 of work at a 50% margin, the overall margin will still be 23% – that's better than you wanted anyway."

Paul admitted that he had never thought about it in those terms. He started using this formula when bidding on contracts, and quickly won a lot of new work.

In 2012, just 12 months after I had joined the business, we received an offer of £10m plus earn-out from a French company that was backed by an American private-equity firm. They had already secured contracts to do maintenance work for the Royal Mail in Scotland and the south of England, so were looking to acquire a company to cover the area in between. This was exactly what Garside & Laycock did.

Paul accepted the deal and went straight out to buy himself a Rolls Royce like Simon Cowell, the music impresario, had. This was something that Paul had promised himself if he ever sold the business. The only downside, he subsequently discovered, was that when he drove around Lytham, everyone thought that it was Simon Cowell. After peering in to see the driver, people were really disappointed when it turned out not to be him.

As for me, I walked away with £1m. My new super non-exec model was really starting to pay off.

Healthcare Communications

I first met Mike Cunningham in 2010 and immediately realised that he possessed all the right characteristics to be successful in business.

Mike wanted to sell his business, Healthcare Communications UK

Limited, which sent text messages to hospital patients reminding them of their appointments and then surveyed their hospital experience afterwards. However, at that point the business wasn't really large enough to be of interest to a buyer. Nevertheless, we stayed in touch and, in 2014, Mike came to see me to explain that he had received an offer for the business.

Now, a key rule in business is to be honest, so I told Mike that I thought the offer he'd received was derisory. Mike was deflated, so asked for my help in securing a better offer. We negotiated a deal and Mike agreed to pay my usual fee – although it was clear that he expected me to work exceptionally hard for it.

Mike had built a strong team around him by using a people expert named Val Brown, who had matched people to jobs where a specific skill set was required. After a year of plugging away, the management team and I had a collective brainwave about expanding the business into sending letters for hospital trusts. It worked a treat and over the next couple of years revenue, and therefore profitability, really took off. We ended up instructing the corporate financiers and accountants, Grant Thornton, to look for a decent-sized, listed company to take over Healthcare and manage its growth.

Mike and I did about nine presentations to potential buyers, which brought in six offers. We nearly sold the business to a publicly listed company, which would have been ideal, but they pulled out. This was a big shock, which resulted in Mike deciding not to sell the business and just carry on growing it instead.

Fortunately, soon after that we received another offer from IMI Mobile plc, which bought Healthcare Communications for a price considerably higher than Mike had originally been tempted by. I ended up with a cheque for a decent amount, and Mike and I parted in the traditional way, by going out on the town to celebrate until the early hours.

My GOLDEN RULES on selling a business

Hire top-quality advisors

Businesses should always trade up. If you have Blackpool lawyers and accountants, you aren't going to look like a big national or international business, but rather like a local, Blackpool business. No one is going to take you seriously.

I don't believe that we would have ever sold Garside & Laycock to a French company, worth €3bn and backed by a New York private-equity firm, if we had been using local accountants that nobody had heard of. It's well worth the extra money to give the right impression.

One size doesn't fit all

Depending on the company, it may be that a trade sale, private-equity investment or stock market float is the best outcome for your business, so consider your options carefully and be flexible.

Tackle any problems your business has early on

Buyers have to be convinced that your business is a good investment. Over the years, I have found that the main reason for a deal failing has been the buyer thinking that after the event, somebody will say, "You bought what? For how much? You must be stupid!" They would rather not do the deal and miss out, than do the deal and look stupid.

Write your presentation as though the buyer already owns the business

If your presentation seems like a pitch your buyer can give to their board, bank or spouse, you will make it easier for them to persuade other people of the value of the sale.

Mini-Cam

I n 2013, my company was introduced to Nigel Wilson and his wife, Janice, who owned a company called Mini-Cam. The business made cameras that, amongst other things, could go down drains and sewers to check for cracks and blockages. Nigel oversaw the manufacturing and sale of the cameras, while Janice looked after the administration of the business. The business was making good sales and profits.

Nigel and Janice had received an offer of £7m for the business. This offer had unfortunately fallen through and Nigel was now unsure how to proceed.

Nigel agreed to take my company on with me acting as a super non-exec, so we began to negotiate my company's fee if the business was sold. Nigel started out by saying that the business was worth £10m, so my company could have a share of anything made over this figure. Then we discussed a complicated ratchet scheme whereby my company's share would not meaningfully kick in until the price hit £12m, but would then increase the more the business was sold for.

Eventually, however, Nigel decided that he would pay a percentage of anything that my company could secure for the business over £15m, a price that he was now hoping to receive. It was quite a jump from the £7m initially offered, but I could see that the business had loads of potential, so I agreed to the deal.

The business did have some strategic issues that needed to be resolved before it could be sold though.

The first issue was that Nigel only manufactured a type of camera that needed to be manually pushed down drains. There was a motorised camera available on the market, which could be driven down a drain and therefore go further, but these were made by an Austrian company and Mini-Cam was only their UK agent, allowed to sell the motorised cameras alongside their own, but in the UK only. Mini-Cam's manual cameras were sold in other parts of the world by a network of distributors, many of whom also sold the Austrian motorised one.

The problem then was that Nigel wanted Mini-Cam to make its own motorised camera, which he was confident would be better value and quality than the Austrian one. However, he knew that if Mini-Cam did that, the Austrian firm would stop supplying it with their own motorised cameras to sell, meaning that Mini-Cam would lose a big chunk of its business before being able to build it back up again with sales of Mini-Cam's own motorised camera.

I talked through all the different possible scenarios with Nigel and we realised that it would require a lot of tact to keep the Austrian business onside while Mini-Cam made the transition from selling their motorised camera to selling its own. In my opinion, Nigel didn't always see eye to eye with his contact at the Austrian company, so we didn't think that approaching him would be very successful. Instead, Nigel and I decided to travel all over the world to visit distributors at the same time as beginning negotiations with the Austrians.

Predictably, these trips involved a fair few evenings out, with one such memorable night being when Nigel and I were in Indianapolis receiving an award for Mini-Cam. After a few drinks in the particularly riotous Tartan Bar, we realised that we'd left the award behind at the ceremony in our enthusiasm to start celebrating. Fortunately, we retrieved it before the organisers found out.

We eventually launched Mini-Cam's own motorised camera, named Proteus, and managed a good enough handover with the Austrian supplier, who set up in the UK to sell their cameras directly – so it all worked out well. It helped that our motorised camera was much better value and quality than the Austrian one, so Mini-Cam beat them hands down in the market and still does to this day.

We also worked hard to generate interest in Mini-Cam, eventually receiving an offer of £25m for the business from a large stock market listed company. But, much to Nigel's distress, the deal collapsed. As a result, Nigel told me that he was ending the arrangement with my company and giving up on the idea of selling the business. Yet I knew that Mini-Cam could be sold and, although Nigel didn't really seem to believe me, I persuaded him to carry on.

We decided that the best way forward would be to sell the business to a private-equity firm. I felt that Nigel would make more money this way, and it would enable him to give some shares to his management team, something that he had always wanted to do.

So, I spent the next six months with Nigel preparing him and Mini-Cam for a private-equity deal. At the beginning, it was hard to imagine Nigel as a private-equity kind of guy, because he was a business owner who had never been in that world; but, after coaching and preparation, Nigel was ready and, between us, we had created a fantastic presentation.

We received many offers from private-equity firms, but Nigel accepted a bid from Lloyds Development Capital, part of Lloyds Bank, and the bid valued the company at £35m, with Nigel receiving a huge sum from the deal on day one. Nigel was then able to invest in the new business, Mini-Cam Enterprises Limited, which was a stunning result for Nigel and Janice.

Fortunately, my company received a considerable sum for its share of the deal too – my next big success.

The two Lloyds Development Capital (LDC) investors, Chris Wright and Johnnie Bell, did ask me what my plans regarding the business were. I told them that I was basically there to help Nigel, but that if they wanted me to have a role in the new company then I'd be happy to do so. Equally, if they didn't want me to join the new company then that was fine.

Chris and Johnnie said that they liked me, but that corporate governance rules meant that they weren't able to appoint me personally to the new business. So they did a big search for a new non-exec chairman and, failing to find one, then phoned me to say they would love me to do the job.

I laughed and replied that that wasn't because LDC wanted me, but rather because they couldn't find anyone else – I teased them about it mercilessly for the next two years.

Regardless, I took on the role and bought a personal stake in the newly formed business. Nigel ran the new business and even worked harder than he had before, because he knew that with private-equity investors on board, the business would be sold for a very large sum.

Having private-equity investors in the new Mini-Cam Enterprises Limited business was initially a bit of a shock. While it had previously just been Nigel, Janice and me working together, there were now two guys from LDC, a finance director, another non-exec, Nigel and me.

Every business owner who goes into a new company with private-equity investors must start off thinking, 'Blimey, what have I done?' because it is a very different way of running a business. But to his credit, Nigel really got into it and continued to listen to my suggestion that he just stay focused on growing the business.

The great thing about having private-equity investors on board is that they are very clear about what they want to achieve – you can't ever accuse them of not outlining their expectations. As long as you deliver on these, everyone is happy. But, if you deviate, change your mind or try to be clever, they will become annoyed.

The LDC team had written an investment thesis for the new company which was brought to every board meeting. They were always thumbing through it and checking that we were doing everything that we had agreed to do at the beginning. Throughout the period, we never rewrote the business plan and just agreed to keep doing what we were doing.

My role as chairman of the new company turned out to include maintaining a good relationship between Nigel, the new finance director, and LDC.

Fortunately, I managed to keep everybody working well together and, in late 2017, we received an offer of £85m for Mini-Cam Enterprises Limited from Halma, a FTSE 250 stock market listed company. The offer was accepted. While LDC and I exited, me with a payment of several million pounds from the sale of my shares, Nigel banked another huge sum and stayed on running the business.

Everyone was happy.

My GOLDEN RULES on getting a private-equity investor

Understand the animal

The old joke about private-equity firms is that they enter every room backwards because they never take their eye off the exit. They are totally exit-focused and, if you are too, the partnership will work.

Be a team

Running a business can be lonely and hard when you are largely dependent upon your own wit. But with private-equity investors on board, you have to be an inclusive team player who keeps no secrets from his investors. If you don't like the idea of this, avoid!

Under-promise, over-deliver and just keep going

The private-equity houses have seen and heard it all before, they have invested in similar businesses and know that the numbers don't lie. Work hard and aim to impress – never drop your guard or take your foot off the gas.

15

Going Forward

uring my time in business, I have been lucky enough to see many exciting beginnings, where businesses start to take shape and come to life, and a lot of successful ends, where the big rewards and glittering prizes are found.

Yet I've come to realise that the most important part of any business journey is the middle, when all the hard work, effort and grind is put in. The middle is often overlooked, as it lacks the glamour of a beginning or end, but the middle is the bit that matters the most – the bit that makes the difference.

It's not surprising that the middle gets so little attention in life though, as most people are rubbish at it and therefore prefer to focus on the beginning or end of any activity or project. In fact, the middle rarely gets a mention.

For example, if we are having a new kitchen fitted, everyone gets excited about the initial stages of planning, where we choose the colour of the units and accessories, and the finishing stages, when we are enthralled by our new kitchen and able to invite friends round to see it. But we get frustrated in the middle section, when the builders are ripping the house apart, dust is everywhere and we're trying to cook yet another meal without a freezer or an oven. During this stage, everything seems to take forever and we begin to wonder why we embarked on the project at all. The middle bit is where we lose momentum: where we say it's too hard and want to give up.

But people successful in business, and indeed life, are the ones who focus on the middle, because that's the part that spells the difference between success and failure. The middle is cold-calling social clubs, it's drilling boards onto reception walls and carrying an enormous metal postbox around with you to meetings – it's hard, painful and lonely. But it requires our attention, because you can't have a fabulous ending without effort in the middle.

Business is all about the middle. If you take one thing away from this book, please take that.

I hope that reading this book has inspired you to look harder at your business model, to focus on your customers more and push through the challenges that you were trying to ignore. To keep going. Success comes from persistence.

To my surprise, writing this book has motivated me too. By looking back at my roller-coaster journey, I've realised that, although I've enjoyed helping other people to grow and sell their businesses, I'm now itching to have another go myself.

So I'm going to start another business of my own. I don't know what it'll be yet, but I know that it will have a cracking business model and the potential to grow.

Right now, there are hundreds of exciting opportunities out there for businesses. Especially with artificial intelligence and technology reshaping our lives, from the way we travel to how we create and use energy. And I don't want to be standing on the outside, I want to be right in the middle of it.

And that's the bottom line. Creating and growing a business is one of the most thrilling things you can do in life, because you aren't just in the stands shouting at the players, you are on the pitch playing the game. You are making a difference. And not just to your own life, but to the lives of all the customers that benefit from your product or service. That's a great feeling.

If you have a good idea, a great business model and some steely determination, go for it. Yes, it'll be hard work and the early starts and late nights will wear you down. And sometimes you will sit at your desk and wonder why you don't just go back to your boring old job, instead of dealing with all the challenges of growing a business.

But, if you stick at it, and keep going through the beginning, middle and end, then the rewards will come. Remember, try to be rich, but not famous – life is better that way. And it's better to be remembered for doing something, than being forgotten for not doing anything.

I wish you all the very best and hope that, whatever you do, you make your mark.

****

I would love to hear from you, so please feel free to get in touch – you can contact me on book@mark.co.uk or via Twitter on @MarkMillsTweets

Lastly, I have written an epilogue which follows in the next chapter. It's very detailed about the whole Cardpoint experience and is for those readers who want a deeper understanding of how I approach business. It's not for everyone and I would only encourage you to read it if you feel that more detail is required. If you do read it, I hope you enjoy it!

Epilogue

This chapter is a more detailed version of the Cardpoint plc story, the business I am best known for.

Please only read this if you are truly interested in, or want more detail on how to succeed in, business. You must also be prepared to read a pretty 'dry' account of the whole Cardpoint story.

I am showcasing Cardpoint because it turned out to be a fantastic business model with multiple facets, many of which can be applied to other businesses. So, look beyond the fact that it's a cash machine company and think about where the various ideas can be implemented within your own business.

Lastly, I have organised this chapter chronologically, explaining first how we found the idea and established the business model, then how the company operated and our exit. These sections all reveal different aspects of the business, so you may find that some areas are more relevant to you and your own goals. Whether you are actively looking for a new business idea, want to increase the profitability of your established business, or are heading for an exit and hoping to realise a lump sum, this chapter will show you how to succeed.

I hope you enjoy it!

Origin of the idea

My brother, Nigel, and I had sold (for the second time!) our postbox business, Postal Facilities Limited. While we had an office with computers, cars and telephones – the perfect set-up – we had no business. Despite discussing the subject extensively, neither of us came up with an idea that excited us, nor one that obeyed enough of our 'rules' to be worth pursuing. Our rules, as previously mentioned, include needing to make money straight away, having a recurring income, being addictive or necessary, location dependent, scalable, sellable and interesting.

To find inspiration, we set off to the US and decided to just walk around. We looked at shops and things for sale, chatted to anybody and everybody to ask about trends, sat in coffee shops and sampled beef jerky, surfed the internet in internet cafés and visited the Post Office. We hired a car and bought petrol (gas), went on a boat trip on the Hudson, read poster adverts and spent hours in bookstores buying books about making a fortune. We went to the cinema, talked to more people and still couldn't find the inspiration we were looking for.

It's no wonder then that, even though I didn't need cash, when I saw a cash machine, or an automated teller machine (ATM), in a corner store, I decided to use my UK card. At that point, we were doing anything and everything to try and find that often illusive thing: a great idea that could be turned into a brilliant business.

I immediately realised a couple of things when the machine asked to charge me $3 to withdraw $50. Firstly, that I had used hundreds of ATMs and had never previously been charged. So that was a concept that piqued my interest – a new version of a familiar service. Secondly, the cash machine was inside a corner store, and I had only ever seen internal ATMs in bank branches back at home.

We chatted to the shop assistant and he told us that the ATM was used often (we felt he didn't want to say too much) and it did help to bring people into the store, which increased sales. He wasn't as clear as this, but we got the message. Interestingly, he mentioned that the store put the money in from the tills – something that I didn't know could happen either.

I noted down the name of the machine and its manufacturer, and we used an internet café to conduct some research. We found that you could buy or lease, for a monthly payment, your own cash machine. The ATM was then connected to the payments network and you kept a percentage of the fees charged. It didn't take long to figure out that, as it costs businesses to bank cash, there was a saving to be had in 'recycling' the money from the tills.

For example, if you are charged 0.5% to bank $1,000, then it's costing you $5 to put the money from your tills into the bank, a cost that reduces your overall profitability. (You are similarly charged for taking payment via credit or debit card, so there is no free-of-charge solution to handling payments – unless you can pay your suppliers in cash and that's basically the velocity of money, but I shan't get into that.)

If, however, you can put that $1,000 into an ATM and dispense it at an average of 20 × $50, then, by charging $3 per withdrawal, your income will be $60 (less your ATM costs – which we will assume are 50% for this example).

Ultimately, your $5 cost of banking $1,000 has turned into a $30 income, giving you a delta of $35. In addition, your ATM is likely to attract people into your store and subsequently increase their spend, as people's propensity to spend grows when they have cash on them. For instance, you are more likely to spend a greater portion of £1,000 if I give it to you in cash, than if I transfer £1,000 to your bank account. Carrying cash empowers and, as the saying goes, 'burns a hole in your pocket'.

The business model

It appeared to me that the retailer experienced multiple benefits in return for very few downsides. The main downside was that the rental of the ATM was typically $199 per month and came, as standard, with a five-year contract. This meant that their commitment was in the order of $12,000.

However, if you work this backwards, at $1.50 net per withdrawal ($3 less the assumed machine costs of $1.50), it would take 8,000 withdrawals over the five-year period to make a profit. As I worked out, that's only 1,600 per year, 31 per week or less than five per day – that's only two in the morning, two in the afternoon and one in the evening. And savings made from not banking cash would lower this break-even point further. Additionally, the increased income the retailer should see would make the payback quicker and the return higher.

In detail, it would look like this:

Thirty withdrawals each week would need $1,500 of cash, saving $7.50 per week or $30 per month. This would mean that the monthly rental of $199 is reduced to $169, and the increase spend of, say, $300 per month (if 30 people spent $10), would deliver about $60 profit on a typical shop margin.

This further reduces the cost of the ATM to $109 per month, which means you wouldn't even need 30 withdrawals each week – the number is probably closer to 22. Therefore, at just over three withdrawals per day, you are heading into positive territory and, at five, you are actually generating contribution. (Bear in mind that, at the beginning, five withdrawals a day would be viewed as only breaking even.)

Pausing the ATM business model for a moment, a key point to note here is that, contained within an action you may habitually, or even just occasionally, carry out, could be the seed of a great idea. As I've shown, whole businesses can be built around reinventing a familiar idea, marketing something from a new angle or simply improving the way in which goods or services are delivered.

Take Amazon as an example. Most of the goods were already for sale, it was the ease of use and mechanism of delivery that turned the retail market on its head. In being able to click on goods and have them delivered straight to your door, cutting out the need to travel to shops etc., I'd bet that we consume more.

I also believe that Jeff Bezos has tapped into what I would call the Christmas Morning effect, i.e., we all like unwrapping presents, even when we know what's inside. I would say that we partly like Amazon because it's like receiving a gift that you can 'unwrap' and enjoy – even if you sent it to yourself!

Thinking about how a service can be improved, especially if it's something that you feel passionate about, is a great starting point for a new business. Maybe there's a cooking ingredient that you find hard to source, a sport that you enjoy but cannot easily hire a court for, or you are convinced that you could improve the quality of furniture and/or how it is bought. Note that I say *starting point* for a great business, you should be aware that a derivative of your frustration may end up being the actual business. So, keep an open mind and allow ideas to flow around you, rather than fixating upon the first version you alight upon.

Back to the ATM business, and armed with the above financial information (I didn't have that many facts to go on, but enough), Nigel and I began to research how to connect a machine to the payments network and what else might be needed. Initially, this was just a telephone line, separate bank accounts and other such standard equipment. We then went on to visit, pretty much all over the world, suppliers of equipment, payment processor providers, Cash in Transit companies and anyone else of relevance. This included some big US ATM operators (including Cardtronics, which eventually bought Cardpoint), and even a few banks, because we thought they might let some secrets slip.

People often ask me about how to meet important people and, to date, I have never found anything more effective than simply asking them – but, as always, with a twist.

Firstly, I truly believe that people in important roles have been helped along the way – I myself have been given help from a variety of sources. If you can tap into the gratitude felt for such help, people will tend to help you.

Secondly, how you approach a person is very important. My children say it's old-fashioned, but I like to write a letter to people – *not* an email. At very little expense, I bought headed paper with my address and telephone number at the top that also says 'From the Office of Mark Mills' (if you want a sample, email me at book@mark.co.uk and I will send you my version to copy). It's on Conqueror paper and certainly looks the part. This investment, in headed paper, envelopes and stamps, makes receipt of the letter alone far more meaningful than any email or telephone call a person may receive, especially given that everybody has a mobile these days and a quick nudge on social media isn't very effective either.

My letter is always very polite, simply explaining that I would be very grateful to spend half an hour with them discussing an idea that may prove mutually beneficial. I outline how I would be willing to travel to them and work around their diary. Finally, I say that I will call them in five or so days to make the arrangements and thank them for taking the time to read my letter.

I don't have a 100% success rate, but responses have been very high. And if somebody writes to me in this way, I have always made time to see them – albeit this takes a little while to organise (if you are already asking Google for printers that sell reams of personalised, headed paper, then this is me setting your expectations – I will see you, gladly, it just takes a bit of diary juggling!). By the way, Tom Hanks uses an actual typewriter to send letters as he collects them. He reckons, and I agree, that people keep those letters for years. I have kept many letters myself, but I've rarely printed an email for posterity.

On this subject, my advice is to be brave and write to anybody and everybody that you would like to be in front of. Don't worry about rejection or looking silly, you have nothing to lose and everything to gain. All I ask is that you don't waste their time; when I have found myself in front of somebody who cannot help and to whom I cannot offer anything, I have said, "Thank you for seeing me, but I don't think we can help each other so I shan't waste any more of your time. But thank you for seeing me, it was very kind."

Continuing with the cash machine business, we were facing three main challenges: there was the issue of equipment (it transpired that we needed approval to connect an ATM in the UK), how to connect to the payments network (we wasted a lot of time trying to figure out how to connect through VISA) and what our business model would be. Whilst I liked the model we had seen, the barriers to entry seemed quite low, i.e., anybody supplying equipment to shops might be able to provide an ATM. As it was, the cash machine was just another product, alongside fridges, photocopiers and tills.

My research, which mainly consisted of using every ATM I could, led me to believe that the main UK bank supplier of ATMs was NCR. I rang them and managed to meet them to discuss equipment. NCR had made fortunes by selling banks 'through the wall' ATMs, like those you see outside banks and supermarkets. They are heavy duty, have large safes and normally need more than a standard telephone line, i.e., they are high cost. They are also available 24 hours a day, giving them high usage levels.

Fortunately, NCR also produced a smaller model, designed to go within bank branches to speed up the withdrawal process – these were also used more during rainy days. NCR's cost for these internal machines was £13,100, which presented a challenge, in terms of the equipment cost, if the retailer was going to be asked to pay for them.

In addition, ATMs in the US were mainly produced by a company called Triton. These machines worked well enough, but did not appear to me to be as robust as the ones in the UK. The Triton machines also didn't look like the ones in the UK, which was equally problematic. If our ATMs were going to charge for withdrawals and the machines were going to be installed in unexpected places, I thought that if they did not look like an ATM that UK users were familiar with, then it would create more barriers to getting our business off the ground.

The NCR version looked and acted like a bank ATM, yet it was smaller. In fact, as I later found out, most people could do a cash withdrawal with their eyes closed, as it's always the same sequence, the buttons are (deliberately) in the same places and even the beeps sound the same (now that I have told you this, try it).

Therefore, my decision was to use NCR equipment.

However, I did still need to address the fact that, mathematically, $199 per month against equipment costing over £13,100 (plus irrecoverable VAT) didn't really add up. My eureka moment came once I'd figured out that we could adapt the business model. So, instead of asking the retailer to contribute towards the cost of the ATM, we decided to place the ATMs in premises at our own cost and just sell the retailer on the fact that extra visitors to their premises, and the amount those visitors spent, would be enough of a benefit to them.

Using this strategy, I worked out that, if we charged £1 per withdrawal and kept the whole amount, alongside depreciating the machine over five years, we would only need 30 withdrawals each day to break-even. I'm now going to breakdown and explain how I arrived at this figure.

First, depreciation is where you split the cost of something over its useful life. Now, accountants reading this may disagree with my simple explanation but, as far as I am concerned, it's the best way to describe it. So, for our ATM business, a machine that cost £13,100 plus VAT = £16,600 (because we could not get the VAT back), and would be written off over five years, i.e., £3,320 per year or £63.84 each week.

Armed with this information, I needed to add on the cost of the cash in the machine (more of this in a minute), as well as the cost of transporting this cash. Each cash delivery was about £80, and we estimated that we would need one every two weeks, so the cost would be £40 per week. There would also be a telephone line, costing £60 per quarter or £4.62 per week, and any maintenance, which I projected would work out at £600 per year or £11.53 per week. All in all, weekly costs would amount to £120.

On top of this was the cost of cash, which we were charged for as though it was an overdraft, i.e., the more we 'drew down', the higher the interest charge, as I explained earlier in this book. The working assumption was that if we needed £25k per fortnight, per machine, then the average balance was £12.5k at a rate of about 5% per annum – equating to £12 per week on interest.

I assumed that we would need another £80 per week for other costs, such as admin, banking, signage and installation, which brought the weekly cost up to £212.

This meant, simply, that we needed 30 withdrawals each day per machine to break-even. This was an easy number to remember, target and calculate everything from, i.e., if we had 20 ATMs, we needed 600 withdrawals each day.

We approached various people about installing machines and were immediately challenged by savvy retailers who said they wanted some of the income. We successfully rebutted this by asking for a contribution to costs – particularly when we explained the rounded up outlay of circa £20k including installation.

We did however agree with most retailers that once we reached 1,000 withdrawals per month on their ATM, we would give them 10p for every withdrawal after that. For example, if their machine had 1,100 withdrawals, the retailer would earn 100 × 10p = £10. This was not a life-changing amount, but it made everybody feel better and when some ATMs reached 2,000 withdrawals every month, this gesture became more meaningful.

Now, it depends on how you view your financial data, but I always worked from the fact that, if there were 30 days in a month and an ATM did 950 withdrawals, I could easily see that we had made profit on that ATM of £50, less a minimal amount of cost.

Later, as I was surrounded by accountants, i.e., when I had a group finance director, a UK finance director, a financial controller, two financial analysts and a team of accountants operating payroll etc., my business model was refined to the 'nth degree' and the costs were so finely tuned that I could see how much each machine contributed every day. I loved this aspect of business, the fact that a really granular, sophisticated financial model could give me complete data transparency – I could clearly see each day how well we were operating.

To extend this further, we built each cash machine its own 'Profit and Loss' account, as though they were all standalone businesses. All costs associated with a machine were then allocated to its account, including any variations specific to it, as well as its income – this meant that by the end of Cardpoint, I had 6,500 mini businesses that I could individually track.

You should always look to expand any business one customer at a time, and always imagine that each one should be treated as if they are your only customer. I did this with every cash machine I owned and it allowed me to view high-performing, break-even and loss-making machines in a simple report. This was a very powerful tool and assisted my decision-making every single day.

In your own business, it's worth figuring out exactly how much each customer costs you: are they high-maintenance and pay slowly, making you carry the cost of their slow payment? How much staff time do they take up and how big is your margin? Over the years, many business owners have been surprised to find that their supposed best customer is costing them money, whilst their slower, lower profile customers are making them their best profits. Be ruthless in your appraisal and don't be afraid to make some assumptions when first building a mini Profit and Loss account for each customer.

To any business owner who is going to be very successful: you cannot underestimate the sheer power of accurate information, particularly when it comes to the finances. In this way, it's enormously satisfying when you start being able to predict how your business will perform each day, week, month and year. Even if you have to teach yourself how to populate an Excel spreadsheet, it's worth doing for the absolute control it provides you with.

At the end of the month, when everything balances and you have updated the forecasts with actual figures, you will begin to act like the most successful business person on the planet. The most thumbed through, amended, annotated and crumpled document on my desk is my business plan. I still write, amend and update one for my own personal use – for example, the costs of writing this book, its projected return and the cost of the launch are all factored in and will be updated.

We became so good at forecasting and planning at Cardpoint that, when we predicted at the beginning of my final year that we would achieve £100m, we managed to hit £98.2m and made a profit of £19.8m against our predication of £20m. This meant that 12 months prior, we predicted to within 1.8% of revenue and 1% of profit our exact earnings.

I always convey this information to business owners who tell me that their business is too volatile to predict. I like to explain that I had little idea who would use our ATMs or how often, if there would be publicity (adverse or not), how many machines might be stolen, how many phone line faults would bring machines down, when the cash in transit people would miss deliveries for security reasons or when a retailer would close their shop. Yet I still managed to take these factors into account *and* subsequently hit the £100m of revenue and £20m profit target, which galvanised the whole company behind me.

How the company operated

The next stage of our business was working out places to put our cash machines. Nigel and I began by driving around, buying lists of retailers, advertising in Forecourt magazine (which was read by petrol station owners), and just generally talking to everyone and trying everywhere we could think of. Pubs and nightclubs were surprisingly rubbish locations, since most of the time they are empty, whereas petrol stations and convenience stores turned out to be good locations – our best customers turned out to be motorway service stations. We were also careful to remember that while the owner of the petrol station was our client, the person withdrawing cash was our customer. In that respect, we had two different audiences, both of which had to be kept happy.

Obtaining new retailers was a numbers game.

We bought lists of retailers in blocks of 10,000 and set about ringing them all. Out of 10,000, you tended to get through to the right person about 30% of the time, meaning you had about 3,000 conversations. That resulted in about 1,000 appointments to discuss the matter further. Typically these meetings had one in three signing up, which gave us about 333 retailers who wanted a machine.

Yet we had our own criteria about each premises' suitability, meaning that when we put retailers to our internal committee, we rejected about two out of three requests. This ultimately meant that we were left with 111 (or 100 for round figures) retailers, from the original list of 10,000, that would have machines installed.

Out of that 100, only 70 would mature as expected, i.e., reach 30 withdrawals per day over a nine-month period. Those other machines, the 30% that we were wrong about, would then be removed.

Overall, this meant that 10,000 retailers would yield 0.7% of successful placements. Knowing these numbers, we were happy once we reached our 70 out of 10,000, but still proceeded to refine and sanitise the list beyond that, deleting anybody entirely unsuitable. And then, guess what? We rang the rest again. And this time, whilst the original number had dropped to about 9,000, we placed a further 50 or so machines. Never be afraid to approach anybody twice if your idea is still suitable for them – just view the first conversation as having warmed them up!

With regard to improving profitability, the main ways to do this were:

We increased the number of machines and the profit margin while reducing the operating costs. It's the same in any business – more customers at a higher price with lower buying costs will see a multiplier effect on your profitability. To that end, we were always placing more machines to increase our overall turnover.

We increased the price of a withdrawal to £1.50, which reduced usage slightly but gave us 50p per withdrawal in clear profit.

We negotiated constantly with our suppliers for better pricing on the machines, as well as on cash deliveries, telephone lines, alarm costs and parts for maintenance, etc. If you do the same, you too will see a greater increase in profitability than you may initially imagine.

While putting the price up was relatively easy, reducing supplier costs was a trickier challenge – until it came to the HBOS acquisition. As we bought 816 high-transacting but non-charging machines, we were suddenly processing about 816 × 9,000 withdrawals per month, i.e., 88m more withdrawals per year plus balance enquiries etc.

As a result, negotiations with our transaction processors became very meaningful, since they obviously wanted to take on that extra volume. We subsequently negotiated for the reduction in processing charges across our whole estate, meaning that the day we swapped everything over, every single machine cost less to run. Naturally, we had to amend each Profit and Loss account to reflect this.

At the same time, we started charging on about one third of the machines, increasing our income exponentially despite transaction volumes dropping. Without going into too much detail, if you use a 'free' machine, your bank pays the machine operator circa 20p for giving you the cash. Therefore, where a machine had been used 9,000 times each month, we only earnt about 20p per withdrawal. But, when we converted machines doing 9,000 withdrawals per month to charging machines, we went from 9,000 × 20p = £1,800, to about 2,000 withdrawals at £1.50 = £3,000.

Not only that, we also reduced our operating costs, as they only needed 2/9 of the cash previously required. Income went up, the cost of the cash we had to put in went down and, as I just explained, so too did the processing costs. All in all, a very profitable acquisition which obeyed all of the rules – increasing the number of customers (machines), with higher income (we put the price up) and lower operating costs (lower processing costs).

Exiting Cardpoint

Since I had consciously kept account of Cardpoint at a granular level, the company was already in great shape when we were approached about selling. Most businesses are in good shape, but to exit you need to have really refined everything and be in precise working order.

There are a million more aspects of Cardpoint that I could go into, but I hope these last 5,000 words have given you a closer look at the particulars. In my next book(!), I may go into even more detail.

Lastly, I am often asked whether my being successful has affected my children. I think it has sometimes been tough on them, because people have been known to say, "it's alright for you, your Dad is rich" and so on. But I believe they have handled it very well and have kept their feet on the ground. Just to make sure though, I did add some disinheriting events into my will.

It was originally done slightly tongue-in-cheek, but as I can't set my children key performance indicators and am unlikely to sack (evict) them if they don't perform, I decided that whilst I am alive they will be disinherited if they do any of the following:

1. Get a tattoo
2. Touch drugs
3. Abuse alcohol
4. Have anything other than Isabella's ears pierced
5. Marry an undesirable (my definition of undesirable will be the one that counts!)
6. Smoke (except for a cigar on Christmas Day!).

My children all know the rules and it's become a source of amusement. For instance, they all egg each other on to get a tattoo, so that instead of inheriting a third of our estate, those remaining would receive half each. Maybe it's a bit harsh, but it's worked so far. I have also emphasised that I will still love them should they choose to get a tattoo, they just won't inherit. Once I'm gone, the kids can do what they like, but until then, they need to follow the rules!